DYING
IS
LIVING

What Happens When We Die?

DYING
IS
LIVING

What Happens When We Die?

TERRY ATKINSON

NEW LIVING PUBLISHERS
164 Radcliffe New Road, Whitefield, Manchester M45 7TU
England

First published 1998

British Library Cataloguing in Publication Data
A catalogue record for this book is available
from the British Library.

ISBN 1 899721 02 9

The King James version of the Bible is used throughout,
unless otherwise stated.
The N.I.V. is the New International Version;
R.S.V. the Revised Standard Version;
A.S.V. the Authorised Standard Version.

Produced and printed in England for
NEW LIVING PUBLISHERS
164 Radcliffe New Road, Whitefield, Manchester M45 7TU by
Gazelle Creative Productions Ltd, Mill Hill, London NW7 3SA.

Contents

*Dedicated to all those who have gone on before,
who were part of the Church terrestial,
but are now part of the Church celestial.
They ran the race with patience, with great endurance
as seeing Him who is invisible and invincible.
They kept the faith, because the faith kept them.*

Introduction

There is a mystery about death. It is shrouded with a deep darkness for so many. A veil had been placed between life and death. Jesus has torn that veil in two, and He has gone to the other side of it as seen in Matthew 27:50,51 and Hebrews 6:19,20. There is light and life in the valley of death for all because the Light of the World has entered into it, and secured it forever by filling it with His presence. Jesus has been there long before you arrive, and that is a pleasing thought. He has been working at its beauty for nearly two thousand years!

The dread of death is produced by unbelief and fear. Its strong hold is the result of sin, and any uncertainty comes from our human understanding of things. Jesus went through death so that real flowers might be planted where everybody would be buried. We live 'in' and 'by' faith, we die as we have lived. We die in hope, we die in faith, we die in the knowledge of the Son of God. These things are more than headstones or a pile of earth heaped up around the grave of a loved one. There are no marble chippings here.

Psalm 23 says literally, 'Though I walk through the valley of shadows, I will fear no evil, for you me.' You might think a mistake has been made by leaving out the words 'death' and 'you are', which are usually placed between 'you' and 'me'. The original language reads as I have written it. There is no mention of death in Psalm 23; the word has been added. There is no 'you are' between the words 'you' and 'me'.[1]

There are glimmers of hope presented to us in the Old Testament, and then brought into full daylight by Jesus Christ in the New Testament.

Commencing in the Old Testament, with the death of people such as Abraham, Moses and Joshua, we even have suggestions from their dying of how God has provided something better for us. Men like Enoch and Elijah are dealt with as they passed into Eternity without dying. Job speaks of having a new body. Abraham became the pioneer of life after death. 'The rod that budded'; the goat turned into the wilderness; the pigeon that was released into the skies; the young children that both Elijah and Elisha raised from the dead; even those who were bitten by

7

snakes found life when in fact they should have been dead. These are seeds which suddenly find their full maturity in the New Testament.

The death and resurrection of Jesus Christ makes all the old promises relevant, and each jot and tittle is fully fulfilled. Jesus Christ is the only one who ever made promises to meet with people beyond the grave, and kept those promises. There are so many records in the New Testament of Jesus appearing to those whom He had promised to meet with, after His death. He is absolute proof that there is living after dying.' Because I live you shall live also.' God is not a God of the dead, and, therefore a dead God, but the living. To use Bible words, He is the God of the 'quick' and the dead.

Dying is Living deals with types and figures, sacrifices and offerings given for your admonition, training and learning. This book is a guided tour right through the New Testament, exploring what is meant by such things as 'Present with the Lord'; Abraham's Bosom; the time of my departure; Paradise; Decease; those who sleep in Jesus; where the body goes to at death; the meaning of the word 'cemetery'; where soul and spirit ascend at departure; and the final chapter deals with being forever with the Lord.

Insights are given, and meanings are birthed anew, which bring us out of a dark corner, and into a bright light. We are drawn to the conclusion that there is corn in the land, although we seem to live in a land of famine. Joseph yet lives, and the brethren have seen him! We have ample evidence of the facts of life after and during death. That which has been a mystery, suddenly is removed in a measure as the reader is initiated into that mystery. We are in the womb, at this moment, awaiting our moment of birth into another world, just as we came into this world, and we were very much alive before we were born.

What has seemed to be just a hole in the ground, is presented as something far more splendid. The moment of death becomes the palace gate of paradise. No passageway is required from the grave. The real character, the soul and spirit of a person, never goes to the grave. The final out-breathing of the body means the next breath we take is the in-breathing of eternal realities. As those under water, and groping in the mud, we arise to take in the air of another world, far more sublime than the slime we now find ourselves abounding in. That which would close upon you as an iron hand and steel fist never touches you, for at the moment of death, you have gone on in life.

Death is not the end, it is not even a beginning, it is a continuation of new life in Jesus Christ. Even in our own world, as the seasons change, it is not the beginning of nature, but the continuation of nature in another form. Life is splendid, life is rich; life, eternal life, is full of diversity, and has a destination of its own.

N.B.

As Christians, we do not just die. We die as we have lived in the Lord. There is more beyond the other side of the grave, than there ever was on this side. We only spend a short time here. Jesus has gone to the other side as our representative, where in the presence of the Father He intercedes for us.

John 21:4 says 'He stood on the shore' as the fishing party came from the sea. What a wonderful picture of coming to the end of our living and fishing. Jesus meeting with us on the shore with a fire burning and a meal cooked.

My youngest brother had tragically drowned in a deep lake and to have had such a book as this would have been a great comfort to me. At that time my knowledge of the Scriptures was as limited as my finances and I had never heard anyone speak of life after death.

My darkness needed turning into light, my reasonable doubts placing beyond all reasonable doubt. As a family we were left with our grief. We were given pamphlet-type reading materials, but the sea was so deep and my boat so small, the grief so painful and the ointment sparse. There appeared no salve for our hurts, no real hope, just a few words of sympathy.

That which lay beyond the grave seemed as wilting as the flowers on the day of the funeral. The coffin offered only the sound of wood as it was being sent into an unknown destiny. The brass plate shone, but it did not reflect an Eternity of light. It offered no smile or song, no message of hope, being without message, sympathy or assurance.

Many writings, under closer examination, seemed to skim the surface. They were only 'on the face of things'. Other volumes gave me a headache and, at times, heartache, seeming to go into endless Dispensations, Doctrine and Debate! This book takes you step by step, across the deep waters of death, and, as you travel, you will find that there is no water at all. Only the wet of the mourners' tears mingled with the tears of joy that

we shed as we are received into our eternal abode. The waters have been
calmed, and every storm has been locked in Davy Jones' Locker.

N.B.   Jesus, who walked on water, has left a sure path of light from this side
of the grave, right into the presence of God. As we arrive there, the waters
are not simply shallow, and we will never have to swim across the
straights between death and life, or take a giant leap for mankind into the
unknown. The waters have all been gathered into the outstretched hand
of Christ on the cross. When he said 'I thirst', all the waters were taken
and used up.

As Israel was commanded to pass through the Red Sea, the waters
parted before them, as the feet of the priests touched those waters. The
waters fled as if touched by the dry hand of drought. To those who were
far behind in the crowd, who could see nothing, the waters were still there.
We are like that as we live in this human life. We are on the edge of the
crowd, but when we arrive at death, we find that it has been dealt with,
struck with an immortal blow by Jesus Christ. What we faced and what
we feared is there no longer. We go through with Jesus Christ, who has
gone before as a Forerunner, as a pioneer, as one searching out the land
for us, as He is seen in Hebrews 6:20.

I have met many people who tell me there is not a lot in the Bible about
life after death. Whenever you hear that statement, do not believe it. A
blind man sees no flowers in the Chelsea Flower Show! To the unedu-
cated the thickest volume of books holds no information. The Bible
abounds with light on the topic of life through death, and our passage
into another world. There are places I go to, and when passing through
those famous historical cities and sights, I receive a brochure. When I
return home at night, it is read, and I wonder if I visited the same place
as described in the glossy sheet. There are so many things that I haven't
seen. Some approach life after death never having really studied Bible
eschatology or truth.

When the caterpillar saw the butterfly go by, he said to his friend, 'One
day you and I will be like that butterfly.' 'Don't be silly,' said his friend,
'that would be an impossibility.' We know it is true, because we have seen
and understand the reality of it. How can that piece of irritating grit
become such a large and beautiful pearl? There·are such beauties in such
common things.

There are 'many infallible proofs', to use the words of Luke as he writes to Theophilus in Acts 1:1. These are no cunningly devised fables. They are part of a more sure word of prophecy. Everything future is part of the 'Yes' and 'Yes', as also Christ is to every promise of God. Much evidence is presented to you in *Dying is Living*, to enable you to thank God for the assurance of life after death.

Where the vision has dimmed, and the faith has become a little weak, then as you read these pages, that which has been pygmy will become giant. Those who have just wondered and guessed it would be all right on the night, find there is bread enough and to spare in the Father's house. It will reassure you of all that Jesus both began to do and teach. Life after death is part of the quintessential teaching of Jesus Christ. He knew and knows more about life beyond the grave, because He is beyond the grave, and he is life beyond it. He came from where he was, that we might go where He is. To resurrect Augustine's words 'He became one of us, that we might become one with Him.'

After reading these pages, you will be filled with a longing to go to that City which has foundations, whose builder and maker is God. There will be a thrill about being a denizen of grace and of heaven. That which has been part of the Church terrestial will become part of the Church celestial. We shall want more of the 'evermore' with the Lord. There will be felt, the emotions of the Queen of Sheba when she saw the magnificence of Solomon's kingdom. 'Only half the truth has been told me of all its grandeur and splendour.' When she saw it all, witnessed it all for herself, there was no more spirit left in her. Heaven and Eternity are breathtaking, the vista is all pleasant, and the future all assured.

NOTE

1. See author's book *Paths of Righteousness in Psalm 23*.

1

Unveiling and Understanding Life After Death

There are so many glimpses of life after death in the Old Testament but, as the gold prospector said, 'You have to know what you are looking for and see what you are gazing at.' There are pictures hung by grace in the gallery of God, pictures taken from the many biblical happenings, little sketches of Paradise after death. In the darkness shines a light of eternal splendour. There are many incidents and illustrations of life after death. Even in plant and tree life there is hope that it should scent water in order that it might live again.[1] Every season has its reason and has something to say. If you listen to the Scriptures you will hear David's harp playing softly as it tells of future things.[2]

We gaze into the history and the happenings recorded in the Bible for our learning and admonition, lifting rock and stone to see what is promised about Eternity. There are times when it is as if we see through a thick veil, but as we look into the New Testament things are more plain. After the shadow, the interference, the suggestion in many of the stories contained under Jewish Law, the New Testament gives the substance. The Living Bible translates Hebrews 3:5, 'Well, Moses did a fine job working in God's House, but he was only a servant and his work was mostly to illustrate and suggest these things that would happen later on.'

Frances Cobb recorded, 'We are as ships with the tide out, waiting for it to come in and for us to sail away. We are an army of believers ready, prepared, waiting for the orders to march, not to conquer but to go back to the home from where we came.' At the moment we are on Safari! We are ambassadors, away from home. The Bible shows pictures of home. Life after death is written into the fine print of every promise ever made. It is written into every leaf, scratched into every rock. Rivers and oceans declare it. We are blessed in that we can see pictures of the resurrection in the Bible, before it happens.

The Alexandrian Liturgy fully expresses every hope which is born because of what is placed in the word of God. 'Assemble them — the dead, O Lord, in green pastures beside still waters, in the paradise of joy, whence grief and sadness and groans are buried.'

There is a catalogue of Heavenly things, beautifully arranged and, as we find the references we find great treasure. Dim eyes begin to see clearly. Those with weak faith are made strong. Doubts about future life are blown away by the very wind of Heaven, turning them into shouts of glory and victory.

Every symbol and type in Scripture is given for our learning and admonition that we might know that the resurrection or existence in a full life after death is not simply a New Order revelation. Job knew that his Redeemer lived, and that one day he would see God in a body of flesh.[3] In the materials and metals of the Israelite forms of worship, you will see flashes of light from Heaven. There was a light within the veil of the Tabernacle[4]. When the High Priest disappeared behind the veil into the Holy of Holies it was into the light of the glory of God.

In the figures of cherubims you will see another order of beings of a Heavenly nature. The light from the golden candlestick will show there is a way through the back of the tent. Even as you eat the bread on the table of shewbread[5] it will tell that there is a greater fellowship, larger than on earth. As Israel travelled stage by stage, urged on by a promise of a better land, so are we urged on as we travel through life. The God of the bush which burned and was not consumed, the God of the rod that budded after it had died[6], is the God of that which outlasts the gaze and the desert sands. As Israel stood on one side of the Red Sea and saw others walking out of it into the land on the other side, so we see such things through the eyes of the Word of God.

Life after death is but a continuation of the life we can have now, but in a new body[7]. It is part of the life of love that you can have in the love of God, balanced perfectly on the promises of God to every tongue, tribe and nation. There is an opening, a passage through death even as the Children of Israel were led out of the wilderness of Sinai into the promised land by Joshua. There are bridges which span the divide between life here and now and life after death. Each word from God is so curved as to fit the soles of our feet as we journey on. Some died reaching forward and looking forward to the Cross of Jesus Christ. We enter our rest, after hearing the words 'Come unto Me all you who are weary and heavy laden' (Matthew 11:28).

The very land of Canaan was not only made up of fierce marauding tribes and valleys with caves, but also of mountain peaks such as Hermon and Tabor, and cities such as Hebron and Jerusalem which were surrounded by mountains. You are on a missionary journey. You are as Abraham travelling from Ur of the Chaldees to Haran and the Promised Land. Paul's missionary journeys depict the life of faith. Abraham believed in a child of promise, a life that was to be born and lived after the death of Sarah's womb[8]. It did happen! It will happen for you as it happened for these. They are not made perfect without us.

There has to be a mixture of developments in your faith. Genesis 1:1,2 says you have a life after death. From the void and formless there comes a new creation, a resurrection, stars, sun, moon, creatures, river and streams all bathed in light. The Garden of Eden has yet to be. There is life after Eden. There are rivers flowing out. Pishon — free flowing; Gihon — that which breaks or rushes forth: Hiddekel — that which is rapid; the Euphrates — the abounding, the abundant river. All these flowed on, granting gold and precious stones. There is that coming from the heart of God which is so precious for you. You go on as a river flowing and do not dry up as land which is denied the hand of rain. Cain kills Abel, but another son is given in his place: 'I have gotten a man from the Lord.'

In Abraham, Moses, Joshua, in all the great leaders, there is a sense of something before and beyond. They were all men of travel and their destinations were not all on earth. They sought those things above and beyond their generation, readily recognising the Architect of the Ages, as Jesus is described in Ephesians 1:9,10. They were men preparing for time before them, a company who believed in resurrection and life after death. They were partakers of it.

Those bitten by the serpent found life after death as they looked at the brazen pole[9]. When the people would have died for lack of water, God provided the water and a new lease of life. Dying of hunger they were fed. Going astray they were led back into a place of plenty and beauty. Israel passed through the Red Sea as a type of death towards land and life on the other side.

There were mountain peaks and promises which they neither reached nor fulfilled. Of those who believed in life after death, Hebrews 11 records, they died in faith, having a more enduring substance and believing they would see Him who is invisible. Having spent all their lives as orphans they were to meet with the Father. The deepening shades of night were turned into the dawn of a new day. Faith converted and conscripted every fear into an army of belief. Such is your substance and hope through Jesus Christ.

Death can be like the walls of Jericho, surrounded and shut up. Yet one blast of the trumpet and those walls fell to reveal the very heart of the city. Such walls fall as we proceed through the Word of God. The Jordan flows at your feet but God parts it and you cross to the other side on dry land. Death is conquered, fear expelled, faith has the victory.

Even Jonah, dear Jonah, the runaway prophet becomes a type of life after death. He died in the stomach of a whale to be vomited up on dry land long after it was thought that he had been buried at sea.[10] Jesus used Jonah as a type of His resurrection from the dead (Matthew 12:40).

Life after death is typified in Isaac

Read Genesis 22:1–12.

Isaac was a brave young man. He was offered by Abraham in death; the knife was raised. He became a type of life after death. He was raised whole — the young man laid on the altar was the same young man who rose from the altar. The young Isaac who went up Mount Moriah also came down that Mount with his father. It was a reunited fellowship. There was no breaking of fellowship in death and there was no place of not hearing his father's voice. Isaac lived on to love, to meditate, to open up old wells and to bless his sons. The New Testament tells us he was a type of the resurrection of Jesus Christ and a type of your death and resurrection (Hebrews 11:17–19). Dying for you can be the laying down, to get up refreshed. What has happened while you have been bound in death has been left in the capable hands of Him who is nearest the altar.

Death is but as a knife raised — the blade never plunged into the flesh. There were no lacerations, no bruising or hurting. It depends whose hand holds the knife! God is in charge! Before Jesus came the knife was not only lifted but plunged deep into humanity, destroying the body. In Jesus comes the beauty of Eternal life. The light is not dimmed into unconsciousness but is turned up by the Light of the World who promises that you shall not walk (stumble around) in darkness. To those who sat in the shadow and region of death, light has sprung up. Through the rock, Jesus Christ, death has been blunted. All the believer sees in death is the glistening blade. There is no pain. It is a rubber dagger! The shining blade acts as a light to lighten the face of God. There is no cutting edge, no searing pain.

In the New Testament those who were dying were spoken of as being at the 'point' of death[11]. The hand that holds it is the hand of Jesus Christ. You live for the Lord and you die in the Lord. The knife does not plunge deep. It never comes within a yard of death. It is only used to sever the bonds of earth as this same knife was used to cut the bonds of Isaac, setting free into a fellowship of love. There were people waiting for him at the bottom of the mountain (Hebrews 11:17–19). In type as in figure he was a shadow of the standing up of believers.

The hand of the father lifted Isaac onto his feet. The hand which held the knife was the very same hand which helped him to stand on his feet. The father then took him through the Promised Land. The father's voice and the father's actions were the first thing Isaac saw when he was raised from the dead. The hand that bound, lifted him up. The hand that laid him low, raised him high. All this is not a type for you but it is the reality of what is promised by Jesus Christ.

The young man had a brand new life. The donkey in Genesis 22:5 was left at the bottom of the mount with its burdens. He was the spared and the resurrected son. He did not taste death as it was, and neither shall we. When he was raised, laughter was raised. Isaac's name means 'Laughter'. God has promised that we shall be heirs and joint heirs[12]. Every thought, word and deed was one of resurrection power. Bound up in order to be slain, he was raised because a substitute ram had been found, wrestling with the thorns and the spiky bush, just as Jesus wore the crown of thorns for mankind[13].

Write 'Jehovah Jireh' on the coffin of every trusting, triumphant saint! Let it be drawn in the spilled tears of every mourner. As you think of the Cross of Jesus Christ on Mount Calvary let it be repeated in your heart, 'As it is seen in the Mount of the Lord.' Let every bunch of flowers spell it out; let it be included in every funeral ceremony; let the digging spade sound out this music!

Life after death is typified in the offering of pigeons

Read Leviticus 14:50–53.

Life and death were presented together. One bird was killed over running water, its blood poured into a bowl. The wings of the other bird were dipped into the blood of the dead bird; the living bird, like a Phoenix, flew from the death scene. It had been held captive by the hand of a man; that hand was released in death and the bird found its way into the heavens, free to be what it had been created to be. The inner sanctum, the inner nature, the real you will be released to fly. The bird touched new heights, as you will when natural life comes to its climax. In this gory scene of death there was a fluttering of wings and an escape into the heavens above. One bird was the old life, the other represents the new life in death. No longer captive, it wings its flight into the vastness of the blue. Built within it is the urge to move upwards. Just like an air bubble trapped beneath the water rises to its own natural sphere. Stained by blood the bird circles and soars. Life flew through the window as a released bird.

The cage has been the human body with its limitations. Its wings were not tired or tied, clipped or folded. The blood into which it had been dipped was no burden, produced no limitations. That blood, as the blood of God's Son, Jesus Christ, was the guarantee of freedom. Written on its wings in red were the words, 'free' and 'alive'. Out of death a life flies in the shape of a pigeon, a carrier pigeon, for it carried with it the hope of the human heart. You can live on after death. Its message is clear, there is life after the rough treatment by human hands.

There is a type and time of departure. You have yet to soar on high. Are you blood stained as this bird was? Do you believe that Jesus died for you? Just its wings touched the emblem of death. The blood of another that had died gave it the opportunity to fly into the heavens. This wasn't a crawling through death, it was flying! Flying higher and higher all the way. It must have felt it was going to die. It had seen what had happened to its friend. So close to death, and yet it lived. A door was left open, an escape route, marked with the blood of another.

One bird knew a coffin in a vessel in which it was killed, while the other flew away. There was the freedom of the running water, that the other winged body had been slain over. It took the message of life and forgiveness with it as it was released into its natural environment. It had been captive until the scene of death. This bird, this part of the double nature, was not buried. One half of the duo died, the other soared into heaven and another destiny. That which was held in the hand escaped to build its nest elsewhere. Death simply added another colour, a colour which had never been visible before. The heart of another bird covered its wing tips.

Out of the house and the leprous conditions flew a bird which was stained with blood forever. It was clean. It carried no corruption. It was flying with the evidence of one life given for another. The power of the leprosy was broken as the bird was set free. It sprang forth as music from a trumpet, as flower from the soil. From corruption there was something beautiful. It does not yet appear what we shall be, but we know when He appears we shall be like Him (1 John 3:2), dressed as a bride to be married. It received another colour, the red of blood at death, that enriched it and gave it the mark of authority, of distinction as it flew away.

From the torn and plucked feathers new life and hope was added.

Life after death is typified by the goat that ran free

Read Leviticus 16:1–22.

Again, there are two natures — two goats. One dies, the other lives. One falls to the ground, the other runs. There is much more land for the goat to cover. The mountain ranges await as it expresses its new-found life, not in wing as with the pigeon, but in the feet of the goat. Everywhere it placed its feet was the evidence of life after death. I should have been killed, but another was killed in my place, as with Jesus and Barabbas. This freedom, as with yours, was based on the death of another.

History tells us that Charles the Second had a whipping boy. Indeed, many of the young princes in history did. If Charles committed any crime then the boy was whipped. The prince was spared. Here is the theology of life after death. Jesus suffered as a criminal that you might be royalty, set free from suffering. The heavy hand of the judgement of God was placed on Him. He who knew no sin was made sin for us. He was the other goat suffering for our 'goatish' nature. Judgement on one became joy to the other.

The whole of another world and life are before the goat. It goes into a place uninhabited, but not inhibited, with a fit man leading the way. Jesus is your fit and fitted man, a Fit Man. A man of opportunity suggesting a timely man. In due time, at the right time God sent Jesus Christ to die for the world, your world[14]. Jesus sets free in death and quickens into life beyond the grave. Humanity was with the dying goat, with hands laid on it, all the weakness of mankind were passed onto it. The Fit Man, the better part, went with the living. The goat which died had two hands laid upon it. It was bound and tethered but then was set free. From the scene of slaughter there was still a life set free by a suitable man.

In life you have known the pressures of the hands which call and demand, the steady squeeze of life which chokes so often; impressions have been made which have almost forced you into their mould. Death can be like that. Life can be cruel, leaning upon us until we feel we cannot breathe, crushed under the burden. There is a setting free, to be what God created you to be. There is a release coming through Christ. There is more green ahead, green pastures of tender love and of rich supply. There are still waters for the goat to drink from in its new-found life.

A fit man, a mature man came out with the old goat nature as it was allowed its freedom. From beneath the feet of the dead goat ran a live goat, running into freedom as the other went into death, carrying with it a message of forgiveness. A hand that chose it gave it life beyond the grave.

Life after death is typified in the rod that budded and blossomed

Read Numbers 17:1–8.

The piece of wood, the almond branch, was dead. It had been cut off, removed from the base of its life. It might have been used as a shepherd's rod or something to lean upon. Placed alongside others, it budded, blossomed and bore fruit. There is a comparison here between the unbeliever and the believer. There are those in death that are like dry old twigs. They have served their purpose, they are gnarled and knotted. Through the power of God and a miracle there is a transformation. Power to produce blossoms and fruit came from within. The secret? It was laid in the presence of God as death. An old stick, as some dead body, was beautified because of the place where it was laid. It found new design, beauty and growth in death. That which was fallen, formless and shapeless suddenly became beautiful; fruitfulness began to appear on its stem.

From within are a variety of colours. There is that which is so adorning, so beautiful, which is called resurrection life, marking it out from every other form of death. This, dear reader, is how your life after death can be presented. To use an old proverb, 'Every singing bird needs a green bough.' What a marvellous sight, a tree, a branch, a fruit branch without roots, its source of life being God, fitted firmly in the hand of God. The very fingers of God, green fingers, grew into blossoms and fruit, causing it to grow up before Him as a tender (sucking) plant. It is God's power and presence which caused it to become a root 'out of' a dry ground. A living branch covered with flowers in the presence of the dead old dry sticks. What a message of the Resurrection, of life after death! This blossom was the only thing to grow in the religion of the Old Testament, apart from the beard and the anger of Moses!

Isaiah depicts Jesus Christ as a root out of a dry ground that becomes the Rose of Sharon[15]. Here was a stick, a rod with a future. Every time you came to God in the future you saw flowers. It became a fruit bowl of resurrection life, to be placed in the heart that you might have hope and consolation in believing. The very colour and scent of it is good. They were surrounded by knops and flowers, which were but shadows and images of the real thing[16].

According to these Scriptures and this happening death is a bunch of flowers, not cut flowers but growing, scented, coloured flowers, shaped like the almond fruit, to be placed forever in the presence of God. God brought it back to what it should have been. The golden heart of God did some ploughing, planting, watering and resurrecting. Dying can be like a perfumed flower head because of Jesus Christ. The stench of death has been removed by the aroma of His conquest — flowers in a wilderness, when the desert blossoms as a rose, settling every argument. When it happens for you, every conflicting thought, word and deed will be finalised, every mouth stopped when God moves into action. Put a flower from this rod in your lapel! Place it in the shroud of all who trust and believe! This rod was so different, just as Christianity is different from every other religion.

'The rod that I shall choose shall live again' (Numbers 17:5). The resurrection, the life after death, was and is a matter of choice. God chooses, and you choose, too. It was the lifting and renewing of a man's name. His generation shall live on forever. The order of priesthood was settled. The rod was placed before the presence of God in the Tabernacle. To be absent from the body is to be present with the Lord[17].

Numbers 17:5, the budding rod, was life after death, resurrection out of complaints. In that one rod were four acts, all four seasons in one. Suddenly it appeared with fruit on it. The seasons were put to sleep while the rod lived. The God who can do that can surely raise the dead! Here is the Almighty working on a bit of old twig, for your sake, to show you it is real. It was an emblem of God's choice. It was the voice of God and the will of God in a resurrection. The nature of God, which is everlasting, was forced into the rod as new sap flowing through it, the life of God in part of a tree. Each rod had a name. Only the rod with Aaron written on it, meaning 'saint', was chosen, and lived again. When they came to those sticks, those branches, each one looking like a grave, a coffin in the dust, they were amazed to see that one had blossomed, had borne fruit. Such is your resurrection and life after death. Unaided by human hand, helped by a Divine design. Here was something colourful, fresher, new. A new order of things. The priesthood of a different sort.

You are not going to be raised as some dead dummy, you are going to bear the fruit of the nature of Jesus Christ throughout Eternity. There will be a certain glory about you. The glory of the stick was both fruit and flower. The glory of the believer is resurrection from the dead. Jesus is both fruit and flower.

Life after death is typified in the child raised from death

Read 1 Kings 17:19–23; 2 Kings 4:18,19,35,36.

Both stories are alike. They illustrate life after death as being raised as a young man, as a child. Elijah stretched himself seven times on the still form of the child. The warm body of a living form was placed over the child like the outstretched wing of a guardian angel. There is the shadow of God's salvation falling across the lifeless form. With hands outstretched, the sign of the cross was made. All the power of the prophetic promise was laid on that still form. Like death, the form of the prophet was placed onto the young form.

The amazing thing is, a new vigorous young man comes from beneath the pile, the pile of the prophet's clothing. There is sunshine and rejoicing after death has done its worst. The curtains were drawn back and the sunshine poured in through a little child who was living. Sunshine shone into the heart again. He was restored through an open door, a new life. What were his memories before death? What were his memories after death? Dying is living, because here it is depicted as going to bed and then being roused and raised by the man whose name suggests 'God is salvation'. There would still be time and room for growth in this new life.

Death may be seen as some accident. 1 Kings 17:22 says he was revived. In 2 Kings 13:21, the same word 'revived' is used of the man who touched the bones of Elisha and was brought back to life. Here we have another picture of life after death. How full the gallery of the heart is when we read God's Word! Hosea 14:7 describes corn being revived. The winds and rain have flattened it and it lays down to die, but the warm air and sunshine lift it up again until its golden crown is seen by all. It is lifted by a hand of sunshine. The breath of another was blown into the little lifeless lad. All Elijah was is given to the child.

To revive, as this child, means to put on a show, a show of life. Revival means God putting on a show. It is God's show. So the resurrection from the dead will be, and so is life after death. You are part of that show. Ephesians 1 says we are glorified in Him, throughout the eternal ages. Life is a stage and we are all players, but so is life after death. The stage is much larger, the production lasts forever. We have ceased to depend on flesh for our existence, we now depend on God. As the man fell onto the bed, so Jesus went into the grave to bring us out of sleep, to awaken to another life beyond the grave. His life, power and vigour covered our lifeless forms. Another one did all the arranging, as the child lay there.

At the moment of death the child was taken to an upper chamber and it was there that the power of God took over from human thinking and doing. Words of faith were spoken. There in that region above, new life was manifested. John 14:1–4 says Jesus has gone to prepare the upper chamber that you might live again, laugh again, breathe, speak, play and rejoice again.

Death need not be the zipping up of the body bag for you, it can be the opening of a door into something quite different. The child is not named, for in death we are all reduced to the same level, even as in life after death we are raised to the same heights.

Life after Death is seen as a young child's body being laid in a bed, the shape of the cross in the outstretched body of Elijah being placed over it. The boy was raised in the shadow of the cross.

As you cease to exist in this world, so you enter into another world of life after death, the new world of the fulfilment of the promises of God. In death we are under the mantle of Jesus. Those who die, die in the Lord.

NOTES

1. Job 14:9.
2. Psalm 45:1; 49:4.
3. Job 19:26.
4. Exodus 35:14; Numbers 4:9.
5. Exodus 25:30.
6. Numbers 17:8.
7. Philippians 3:21.
8. Romans 4:19.
9. Numbers 21:9.
10. Jonah 1:17; 2:10.
11. Mark 5:23; John 4:47.
12. Romans 8:17; Ephesians 3:6.
13. Matthew 27:29.
14. Galatians 3:13; 4:4.
15. Isaiah 53:1–3.
16. Exodus 25:31–34.
17. See Chapter 5.

2

Did the Old Testament Patriarchs Live On After Dying?

Each life in the Old Testament draws as a pen an opening from the grave into something more. People were buried in the earth, but in that earth was a sure foundation of a future with God and in God. The grave to them was an outstretched hand filled with good things and with a finger pointing into the future. To some it was a hand filled with thorns, but to the Patriarchs it was a hand that was warm and welcoming. Dying was simply God laying a garment over earthly bodies, as one might cover a diamond with rare silk. The hand of God was full of dexterity, one object being placed in the darkness and another quite different being produced from under the darkness of death. It was sometimes the story of the little piece of grit, entering the oyster's dark shell, to be reproduced as a fine large pearl of great worth.

Each one of the apostles of the Old Covenant, who has died in faith, carried a candle with them into the darkness, and from that flickering, silvery light, we are led to Christ who becomes the Light of every world. He is the light at the end of the tunnel, but in death, He is in the tunnel, at the beginning and at the ending, for He is Alpha and Omega.

There is a form of belief, preached throughout the Old Testament and seen in shadows, figures, types and ceremonies. When all is quiet and still, there is a certain gentle whispering breeze of zephyr proportions, telling us, calling us who will follow them that all is well, all has been arranged.

Jesus Christ simply validated every Old Testament promise, changing type into truth, figure into fact and shadow into substance. This truth of living after dying had to be illustrated, as other principles of spirituality are, through men like Enoch, Abraham, Moses, Aaron and Joshua, Elijah and Elisha. From each, there is a light which shines right through the valley of the shadow of death and an echo which carries to the other side. When Pilgrim in *Pilgrim's Progress* came to the Valley of Death, it all seemed dark, but when he arrived and went through it, there was light all the way[1]. It is like the aeroplane coming to land on the runway at night. As it descends from one world to another, there are lights which all move into one straight line, to guide the machine coming in from another country. As Scripture is added to Scripture, and life is added to the life of the patriarch, their lives act as one great prophecy of future living. Yes, our approach on this side is dark, but all is light as we enter into it. We discover all things have worked together for good.

Abraham looked for an eternal city with foundations

The illustration of life after death is found in Genesis 23:2–20, and Hebrews 11:8–10, when Abraham purchased the field of Macpelah and was buried there.

Every Jew believed he went at death to the Bosom of Abraham[2]. Abraham appeared long after he had died in the New Testament[3]. Abraham is the father of us all. We walk as Christians in the footsteps of Abraham. As he went through life and then through death as a door into eternal life, so shall we as we believe. His footsteps move from the sands of time onto the rocks of true riches in Christ.

Hebrews 11:10 says, he sought a city with foundations whose builder and maker was God. It was something ready prepared. We know he never found that city in the Promised Land, for he constantly lived in tents and built altars. It was a certain city 'Whose maker — public worker — is God'. The 'Builder', its artificer, is God. From the Greek word given as builder we obtain our English words technic, technical, architect and builder. God had not only planned it, drawn it, but built it. All Abraham had to do was to believe that God as a faithful creator would provide it. The maker is the builder and the builder is the planner, the drawer. It is one who does things by the rules of art. Archbishop Trench states, 'This brings out the artistic side of God. It means a person with a trade, craft or skill.'

It is death that God uses to demonstrate his ability in providing a city which finds its echo in John 14:1–3: My Father's house, mansion, place of rest. Before you were born, your parents arranged a house for you to live in. You were born into that which you had no part in preparing. Dying with God is a birth into that prepared by Jesus in John 14:1, 'I go to prepare a place for you.' Death is used to illustrate God's greatest triumph, until you can say O, death where is your sting? Where are your secure doors now? The bright twinkle of light from the eye of God has banished the darkness. The burning bush has been placed there to give all hope in death.

In Genesis 23:7–20, we have forward-looking Abraham buying a field in which to bury his family, and where he also would be buried on the termination of his life in this world. We all know that termination is not extinction, neither is it an end. It is just a turning around. I have often purchased a ticket, and said, 'I want to go beyond the terminus.'

It was Ephron's field in Macpelah which Abraham purchased with silver, which was part of the redemption money of bartering. There was a cave in the field. It wasn't just a furrow they were buried in. There was a certain depth and security in this field. 'Ephron' means 'young at heart'. It is that which is swift and sure. You can be surer in death than in life. 'Ephron' can also suggest strength. There is nothing weak about dying in Jesus Christ. The Lord who sustains all things and upholds all things by the word of his power, is well able to support all in death, when all around has rotted away into nothing. When you face the open grave, a gem in Jesus has been unearthed. There is that faith and hope which a gravedigger's spade cannot cover.

Macpelah means 'the double doored'. There was a way in and there was a way out. There was a door at the other end. It wasn't a cave in the normal sense with thick walls and darkness prevailing. You don't mind entering into anything if you know there is a way out at the other end. There was a way through this cave as there is through death. Jesus has rolled the stone away. There is a gap, which like the door in Noah's ark can admit small and great. Blessed be that man who discovered holes in thick walls and called them doors. Everyone, it does not matter how great or rich, must pass through this one door of death, and then onto and into eternal reality of this before us. We will all know the door into death, but we must know the second door which provides a way out. Jesus said in John 10, 'My sheep go in and out and find pasture'.

We go to the place where Hebrews 6:20 says, 'The Forerunner has gone before us'. Jesus is called the 'Forerunner' in Hebrews 6:20, in Greek *prodromos*. The word Forerunner was used of Macedonian troops who were sent to spy out the land, a little after the similitude of our Commandoes.

They were the Elite Force. It is the word in the Septuagint version which describes first grapes or the first ripe fig. There was a small boat called the Anchora, which was sent out into the fog to reach a larger vessel. Then it had to take its cable, and bring it to the shore, so that the larger vessel was pulled into the port by the cable the smaller Anchora had brought. There was a man in the Anchora who sailed out into the rough waters to guide the larger ship into the port, and his name was 'Anchorarius', one in charge of the anchor. Jesus is our Anchorarius and Forerunner, having entered into the heavenlies for us. The Romans called a man's last gasp his final hope 'anchora sacra'.

The same word placed as Macpelah is used in Exodus 28:16, describing the High Priest's breastplate which had to be doubled. It also describes the curtains of the tabernacle which at the corners and at the entrance with the back of the tent had to be doubled. We all need that something extra in death, and it is called life. This cloth was for extra use, and it gave extra length when needed. At death, we need to be wrapped in that same embroidered silk as Jesus Christ. Jesus has provided the extra mile at the end of life's journey.

Young's *Analytical Concordance* gives the meaning of Macpelah as a spiral staircase. That which commences at ground level, or below the ground, like the one of the New York skyscrapers, and rises far into the heavens. It is not a ladder down, but a ladder up, as Jacob saw, but not with angels ascending and descending, but with saints ascending at death into their eternal abode[4]. It is illustrated here, by Abram — the Father of Heights. C. S. Lewis in one of his famous stories depicts children going into a wooden wardrobe, almost the shape of a coffin, but in it there is a magic door, which leads out into life and adventure. Through that door, they entered into another splendid world.

The ancient versions translate Macpelah 'the double cave' from the word 'Kaphal'. A cove for dying and a cave for living. A man in a stormy sea is about to be destroyed, the waves are going to sink his vessel. He manages to get to a cave in the rocks, and when he enters it, he not only finds a refuge, but a hole in the back of the cave which leads into the king's palace.

A. Maclaren wrote, 'The grave has a door on the inner side. Jesus has the keys to it. The keys of death and hades are in his hands.' John Bunyan wrote, 'Death is but a passage out of prison into a palace.' It is never from a palace to a prison. It is never from living to dying. Jesus has introduced the reverse side of life, which is better than the side you know or have known. When Abraham came to depart it wasn't as Elijah in a chariot of fire.

It says in Genesis 25:8, 'He was gathered unto his people.' Gathered as a bunch of flowers. Gathered as twigs from a tree. Gathered as a child might gather daisies to make a daisy chain. When all has fallen apart or been broken, to be gathered up again, and set in such an order of beauty and dignity. Taken as little pieces of broken pottery and turned into a valuable vase. Rubbed out and re-drawn. Taken and used as a brooch, being placed on a dress or in some other prominent place. To come to the end and find it is a beginning. It is reaching into the dark and finding a sure hand, the hand of a Friend there to help you, and to describe the way. To find that which had faded and fallen like the petal of a flower is gathered to appear again in a new order of beauty, to find that the common daisy had become a rare bloom. He did not fall, he did not slip, he was not pushed off the edge into the dark and onto the rocks below. There was a gathering by a sacred hand. It was the Owner calling and collecting that which belongs to Him.

The same word, here rendered 'gathered', is used for the gathering of sheep by the shepherd. At death, we may feel they have wandered through a thorny hedge. They have gone to the sharp teeth of lion, bear and wolf. They may seem to be out in the cold and on the frosty hills, but no, they rest as sheep in the shepherd's fold. In dying, He has found them and brought them safely home rejoicing. Gathering is to be put together again, just as we are in the resurrection from the dead[5]. In Proverbs 27:25, it is the word used for gathering herbs and spices. It will be the gathering of the sheep, of the soldier, of the saints — the gathering of the people shall be unto Him.

Please note all the worthies that were buried in Macpelah: Sarah, Abraham, Rebekah, Leah, Jacob. We can repeat Isaac Watts hymn: 'When I can read my title clear to mansions in the skies, I'll bid farewell to every fear and wipe my weeping eyes.' Abraham went into death with about as much fear as a lion has of a fly.

Moses at death received the kiss of life

Deuteronomy 34:1–12 is the recorded death of Moses. He died by the word of the Lord. It was the same word he had lived by. The Rabbis and some old translators render the words, 'He died by the word of the Lord' as 'He died according to the mouth of the Lord.' There is the suggestion that God kissed him in death. Just as Nelson asked Hardy to kiss him in death, God kissed Moses, making death like the planting of a kiss. At the end, after life's struggles, God meets with him and kisses him. What a way to die! What a welcome awaits those who are in love with God! Challenged and changed, then kissed at the end. As if two long lost friends have met together at last. Life lined with love.

There was no need to write a long speech or have a long heart-rending wander down memory lane. It simply says God kissed him to death. It was the most holy kiss anyone could be greeted with. The kiss said it all. Worth its weight in gold and more eloquent than the silver tongue. I seal this life with a kiss. God sealed this love affair.

What a wonderful scene — God the only mourner, the only attendant. He does not bring flowers or richly decorated bouquets, but kisses, tokens of love and everlasting love. He does not tie the box with a ribbon, but with a lingering kiss. There was no saying of Mass, no lighting of candles, no ceremony, just Moses and his God. He was brought to the heights of Pisgah, the place of fragrance. There is no stench of death, only perfume. It is a kiss and not a tear which God gives as Moses is called higher than a mountain. Death brings you, as it brought Moses, so near to God, so near that God could kiss him. The expression of deep love is placed upon him as a final act of grace. The action of God went beyond the law. All the greatness and gentleness, all the seriousness of God is introduced with a kiss. A kiss introduces this servant into eternity — the place of kisses and love. Heaven will be the centre of a kiss. It is where all is one, as when lips meet together.

The Rabbis believed and wrote that God kissed Moses to death, drawing the very life from him. They base their facts on the words 'He died by the mouth of the Lord'. The God that breathed into Adam the breath of life[6], now kisses that life out of Moses, as he is taken to the centre of the kiss. Of the 903 ways to die, the Rabbinical teachings say this is the best. Life came to an end in the comfort of a kiss, a kiss of choice. It was the kiss received by the child from the lips of the father when reaching the top of the stairs at night time. The kiss which gives assurance and tells you not to fear. The young child is entering the school gates for the first time. Joined together forever by a kiss. The kiss that says all is well as the child lays in the bed and sees the smiling face. Kisses are a true mark of trust and tenderness. The God of belching Sinai and the bush that burned with fire approaches His loved ones with a kiss — it is all reduced to a kiss. Lovers kiss goodbye, but God welcomes with a kiss. Fear death and the darkness of death as much as you would fear a kiss, dear reader. The promises of God concerning life after death surround us like kisses.

C. H. Spurgeon, speaking to his students on death spoke these words: 'What lovely gems are washed up by the waves of Jordan.' The word of the Lord, and the Lord of the word had arranged it all. A life's work was represented in a kiss.

The story is told that when Leonardo da Vinci was about to die, the king visited him. As they talked, Da Vinci died in the arms of the king. The love of God for Moses and for you was not all used up during his earthly life. There was still one kiss left, and it was the best, kept until the last. All the hurts of life and the pains, the long journey and the suffering were kissed away in death by God. God clave a hollow in the mountain top, to bury Moses in, and that hollow was a kiss.

Moses was 120 when he died. Many years later, during the ministry of Jesus, he appeared again, alive and well[7]. He possessed all the faculties he had possessed as a human being. He has greater knowledge for he knows in advance of the death of Jesus. The Monks of Wiltshire, some eight hundred years ago, expressed our departing beautifully:

> 'God be in my head and in my understanding.
> God be in my eyes and in my looking.
> God be in my mouth and in my speaking.
> God be in my heart and in my thinking.
> God be at my end and my departing.'

May He be there with kisses instead of fading flowers. Eternal life for Moses, as for you, begins with a smile, with smiling eyes, with a breath, with a presence, the presence of God. He died to live in God's presence.

Aaron met with God at the top of the mountain

He died by the word of the Lord in Numbers 20:25, and he had a whole mountain before him as a figure of eternity when he died. Death was spoken of as a going to the top of the mountain. Aaron didn't go through a Valley of Shadows, but to a mountain top. We take and make a marble slab as an epitaph, but God uses a mountain of rock. He reached the top. The body goes to the bottom, it sinks, because it cannot swim through the grave. It goes to be the honoured guest of worms at their banquet. The real you, soul and spirit which make up your character, goes to the top. Death came like a huge mountain, something he had never climbed before. The whole thing was like a great open grave, but each step he took was upward. When he began at the bottom, a way opened up before him, and God was at the other end of the black, huge shape.

God was found hiding himself in the shadows, ready to reveal himself when needed. The last thing Aaron met in death was not death, but God. Not God with a law or with a stick to beat with, but a God reaching out to take him as a prodigal returning. He came to the side of God, as if part of God had been missing while this saint of God was on earth. In death, he reached his other side, and it was God himself. There is no end in God, only new beginnings. Maybe (speaking poetically), he heard the words again, 'You have dwelt on this mountain long enough, turn and go' southwards — to the land of soft, refreshing breezes, the land, the hiding and playing place of the summer sun.

Aaron didn't have to chisel the mountain away piece by piece, boulder by boulder or carry it little by little into another area. There was no taking of it, and casting it into the Red Sea or the Jordan. It was just a straight climb with Moses and his son. From all the shapes and shadows of that great mountain God stepped to welcome home this saint of the Lord. All the High Priest had to do was to walk. The only rest area and the flat part was when he met with God.

Your life might have been a mountain climb. It was a walk, which was seemingly uphill, but at the end of it was God himself. Death was like a great mountain, but it revealed the presence of God. The doorway to eternity was there at the top. God decided when he had walked long enough, and took him into Himself to give him rest and shelter for ever more. As God said to Enoch who walked with God, 'You have walked long enough with me, you had better come into my home.' There was a cabin, a climber's refuge shed or hut on this mountainside, but it was in the shape of God.

We only climb for so long, and no longer. There is a post, there is an end to our ascending, and it is there that God meets with His servant. The death which appeared like a mountain to climb was the very mountain on which God met with the saint of the Lord. Hidden in the rock, there was longsuffering, mercy, peace, forgiveness, kindness — the whole nature of God was here to help him along, appearing as a rare flower perfumed and in full colour. Aaron had never seen the shape of God. He had only seen Him in Shekinah glory. That same nature, those same attributes, are laid at your feet for your use.

When Jesus said, Lo, I am with you always, that didn't just mean this life. There is no limit to the care of God. There is no hedge to the love of God. There is no full stop to God's message of love. What flowed over the banks at Calvary will flow right through into eternity. Where snow had settled, and sun had done its converting work, where the winds had cut and slashed, there God was waiting to welcome the man of God.

Earth's glories dim in heaven's light. What he had been or not been, his failures and successes were all left behind. The laughter of earth was lost in the love of heaven. The joy of the journey, if there had been any, was matured into limitless pleasures, sweet and kind, which are at the right hand of God forevermore[8]. More pleasure than I can measure, the everlasting nature of God is forwarding pleasure. More pleasing than pleasure, much more than any earthly treasure.

Aaron was going to where the rare blooms grow on the top of a mountain. Rare blooms are found here. He reached such a height in death which he never attained in this life. God lifted him as some rare thing, and placed him on a mountain as the showcase for one of his great masterpieces.

When Mary Wilson, the wife of a former British Prime Minister was asked what she would do when her husband retired, she replied, 'I will weave all the happenings of life together into a cloth of gold and wear them in the long cool evenings of retirement.' We take with us what we have been. We are at the end what we have allowed God to make us.

A chamber was reputed to be haunted and a family feared to enter it. The father decided to kill the myth and sleep in it. During the long night, there were no creaks, groans or moans, there were no loud bumps in the night. The only moving thing was the sleeping lungs of the father. By sleeping there he broke the power of it forever. Jesus did this when he entered death, and moved into resurrection for you. That mountain Aaron had to climb has become a mere speck of dust in Jesus Christ, ground into fine sand, and made into clear glass for all to see heaven through. We are at the top the moment we leave this life. This climber had often wondered what was at the top of the mountain, just as you have thought, 'I wonder what is in death?' God was there waiting as Friend for friend.

Deuteronomy 10:6 and 32:50 says he came to the place of the altar (Moserah); it can mean the stall, the cattle shed, the place where after ploughing the harness is taken away. It is the end of a journey. In the New Testament, Paul uses the same thought of death and frames it in this picturesque word in 2 Timothy 4:6, 'The time of my "departure" is at hand.' The word 'departure' was used of unyoking the animal from the shafts or the cart. It was used of lifting the yoke from the neck of the working beast.

In Numbers 20:26, this one was gathered by Him who gathers the waters together, the stars and the clouds are gathered in the palm of His hand. What security! What safety! What strength is going to be yours. You who have been in the heart of God through Jesus Christ are going to the hand of God. The helping hand over the stile.

In Genesis 29:3, this word 'gathered' is used of taking sheep from a wilderness journey, and gathering them as a flock by quiet waters and green meadows, where spirits are as free as sheep in the green. It is into Psalm 23[9]. In Leviticus 23:39, it describes hand-gathered fruit to be placed securely in a basket. It is the gathering together of the fish of the sea. It describes the gathering of children, tongue, tribe and nation, even in 1 Chronicles 23:2 of the gathering together of princes. All these things take place in the book of Revelation[10].

Heaven is to feel a presence, and to discover it is God's presence. It is to feel a helping hand, and find it is God's hand. To see a face, and to know it is the face of God. A little girl of six was ill. She was heard to say what we sometimes feel who are longing for heaven, and even more, the God of heaven, our Jehovah Shamah, the Lord is there. The infant said, 'I wish I was living and well.' For this one departing it was starting. He is both well and living in the land of the living.

Joshua was buried in sunshine

Many have seen death as darkness, and the entering into the grave as some remote hole and castle of despair. This was not so for Joshua in the Old Testament, and neither is it the stated fact for believers. He was not covered with earth or with a gravedigger's spade. The sceptre of God was over every part of his life, for it was long enough to reach to the other side. The gap between life and death was not only made but measured. He was laid to rest in that which suggests sunshine forevermore, in Joshua 19:49–51. *Timnath-sera* — 'the place of sunshine'.

To be bathed, robed and washed in that glittering golden light for the rest of your living. Dying is not the setting of the sun, but the sun rising in all its splendour and fullness of design, shining, spreading, glowing, it is not the covering of the sundial with a cloth of black. It is the rising of the sun in splendour and fullness. Sunshine is an emblem of conquering, happiness, cheerfulness, joy and peace, a radiancy for ever and ever. It is to have a future woven in light.

God uses light as we use fabrics and objects of stone, steel, copper or wood. The sun shining on you as if you were the only flower in the universe. It is the sun which opens up plants and flowers to their full maturity, and eternity is going to do that for you. This life is in the shade and shadows. This life has been a dark cloud and a misty existence. It is digging, while future life is the finding of what we are looking for. Joshua found a place in the sun.

Life after death was a real holiday, a real holy day. There is that which is golden and glorious forever. Buried in a grave of sunshine, wrapped in a shroud of sunshine with flowers of sunshine, arranged with their sunny disposition. Life after death, to use an American expression, is the sunny side up. A coffin, not of wood, but of sunshine. He went to the land where the sun rises first because it never sets. Norway is known as the Land of the Midnight Sun. There is one part of Africa which is known as the land where the sun shines first. The proverb of the ancients declares 'all sunshine makes a desert'. Here, it forms a departure and a destiny.

Even after death Joshua is still Joshua, Moses is still Moses, Elijah is still called Elijah. Nothing is changed in the sense that we still have the same name, and still respond to the same call. We can still enjoy laughter and joy which is as a spring let loose, sunshine and pleasure. This is the believer's real treasure of pleasure. To be set free as the sun in its orbit, described in Scripture as a strong man ready to run a race, or as a chariot in its circuit. The sun is a firm figure of that which never ends. Its beauty shines as some radiant torch. It may sit to set, but it awaits to rise as if it has never disappeared. Like those who go from us, it appears again, just as if it only disappeared to receive a new frame. We shall have a new resurrection body, which will shine as the sun and the stars (see 1 Corinthians 15).

The death and burial of Joshua is so unlike the graves in the New Testament which were whitewashed and full of dead men's bones. Here was one that was bathed in sunshine. Gloom, doom and uncertainty in Joshua became sunshine. The record of his death is found in Joshua 19:49–51; 24:29–31; Judges 2:8,9. He was buried in Timnath-sera, Joshua 19:50; 24:30. The place of the sun. His death was the placing of Joshua in that sun. It was part of his inheritance.

Dr Donald Grey Barnhouse was returning from the funeral service of his first wife and he sought to comfort his grieving children. He asked them gently as a large lorry swept by them, 'Would you rather be run over by a truck or by its shadow?' 'It's shadow,' they replied, 'because that cannot hurt us.' Wherever there is a shadow there is sunshine close by. If you stand with the sun before you, as in death, all the shadows fall behind you. The past is with the past, and the future is with the future. Death may appear as a blot, blank or a shadow, but Jesus is the sunshine of my life and the ending of my strife.

Where I live in Lancashire, there is a local place called 'Sunny Bank', and every grave is just that in Jesus Christ, because hope displaces despair. It is only a valley of shadows that we think we are called to pass through when we die, but when Pilgrim came to it in *Pilgrim's Progress*, there was sunshine all the way. In John 20 and Mark 16:2, we are told that Jesus came to the disciples after the resurrection, and the sun was shining.

There is the seed thought contained in the word *Timnath-sera* of the extra portion. Joshua received something in death that he never had in life. There was the other dimension awaiting him bathed in the light of sunshine. Joshua was the son of Nun, meaning 'perpetuity' — forever and ever. Death may appear as a shroud or a cloud to some, but to the trusting heart, there is sunshine as the hand of God sweeps away the cloud. Jesus died wrapped in the blackest cloud ever, that we might enter into sunshine[11]. He might have died in blackness, but when He arose from the dead it was into beautiful sunshine.

Joshua 15:10 says Joshua went to Beth-shemesh, the house of the sun. Fancy having walls, windows, doors and staircase, rooms and furniture all made out of sunshine. You breath in and it is sunshine. One describing their conversion said, 'It was as if I had swallowed sunshine.' In death sunshine swallows us. Sunshine is the nearest thing to heaven. It is used poetically of our future state, because our minds are all square, and we cannot accept the curve of what God is saying to them. We cannot interpret Divine promises with human wisdom alone. If we do, we look at jewel quality through a glass eye. God uses an everyday thing such as sunshine, because we can identify with beams of sunlight. Can you grasp the concept of having a life form built out of sunshine? Every word, wish, thought or deed is sunshine. 'The sun shall not smite them by day.'

In 1 Peter 1:4 Peter says, like sunshine our inheritance will not fade away. It will never set or disappear. Peter uses the Greek word 'amarantos', which describes a plant which is evergreen and does not fade or die. 1 Corinthians 13:8 says 'love never fails'. Love is the nature of our God. Queen Victoria of England reigned over an empire on which the sun never set. King Louis 14th of France was known as the Sun King. The Irish refer to their banner as a burst of sun. All these things are a reality in Jesus Christ, and come to pass as the believer passes from this limp life to a life of adorable love.

Psalm 56:13 (King James Version) says 'That I may walk before God in the light of the living.' Another translation puts it like this, 'That I might live, ever mindful of God, in the sunshine of my life.' As in life, so in death, the sunshine increases until there are no shadows. Heaven is a record of the happy hours.

John Bunyan brings out this truth of being in sunshine when he penned the words, describing Christians' Celestial City, 'The sun in the city shone both "day" and "night".' The light of that city was as the shining of the sun.

John Gill in his commentary on the Bible writes of Timnath-sera, 'He built it and fitted it for his own habitation and for that of his family.' Albert Barnes in his commentary on the Scriptures says, 'Judges 2:9, the name of the place is also written Timnath-heres, by a transposition of letters. The Rabbinical explanation is that the name, meaning "portion of the sun" was given because the sun was fixed as an emblem on his tomb to commemorate Joshua's command to make the sun stand still.' The record of his achievements went with him at death, but he being dead, is still speaking.

The meaning of the sun and sunshine is ministrant, that which serves and ministers to needs. It brings healing to the wounded spirit. It waits on forever and ceases to function never. All the capabilities, all the wisdom and knowledge, all the power and Lordship of Jesus Christ is going to work on your behalf. The mother makes sure the child rests in complete comfort. For these pale, unhealthy looking bodies of ours, this is our sanatorium. Sunshine is going to be your last stopping place. Sunshine is going to be part of you as the nature and substance of the resurrection.

Joshua died, and went to the God who performed that great miracle of making the sun stand still, while the battle raged[12]. At death, he was buried in that which was named as a great victory, 'The battle of the sun.' When any who trust in Jesus Christ die, they enter into that fullness of inheritance of light as found in the book of Ephesians[13]. They enter into the greatest victory ever wrought by Jesus Christ on the cross. They step from the shadows of this life into the sunshine of another form of life in Jesus Christ. Jesus may have not promised you sunshine all the way, but he did promise it at the end of the way. The Sun of Righteousness has risen with healing in His wings. That means sunshine for your dark clouds. What Joshua was buried in as a type, we shall have in Jesus in reality. The plastic and the plasticine of death will be turned into the real thing in the endless radiancy of God.

NOTES

1. *Pilgrim's Progress*, written by John Bunyan.

2. Luke 16:22,23.

3. John 8:58; Luke 13:28; 16:24.

4. Genesis 28:12.

5. 1 Thessalonians 4:17; 1 Corinthians 15:38–54.

6. Genesis 2:7; 7:22.

7. Matthew 17:3; Luke 9:30.

8. Psalm 16:11.

9. See author's book, *Paths of Righteousness in Psalm 23.*
10. Revelation 1:5,6; 5:10.
11. Matthew 27:45; Luke 23:45; Mark 15:33.
12. Joshua 10:12,13.
13. Ephesians 1:11,14,18.

3

What Happens When We Die?

The Apostle Paul is about to die. He is ready to be offered as a sacrifice should that be necessary. In Philippians 1:23, he says, 'I am between two stoops. I am like a ship riding at anchor as the tide rises, pulled one way and then another. Part of me wants to go, the other part wants to stay.' Does this describe your attitude towards death? There is a certain word Paul uses of his going out of the world which enlightens and makes us realise that death is not a falling apart or a breaking of what we have been for a lifetime when we are placed into the grave. Death is never the end. It is a never-ending ending. It is a new beginning as we step out of the mud and into the palace silver.

'Analusis' is a sailing away

One of the early Christians died and etched on a piece of slate above his grave was the word 'Analusis'. 'Analusis' is the Greek word for departure, and is the same twin word that the Apostle uses to describe future life after that departure. It describes the new world. Within its orb and sound was the ringing of celestial bells. The phrase said it all, explained it all. It is the figure of the ship as the anchor is raised, the rising tide beckoning with its watery fingers in the waves and using the tide as it sails to new worlds of discovery. It is the same verbal expression which aptly describes Paul and every believer leaving the world.

It is the word used for the pouring out of a libation, describing the content of the drink offering as it is poured out. It majestically describes the leaving of this world, having lived a useful life, going out as a sacrificial offering. What a word for every missionary martyr! It was so offered after a feast or other great meal. My life has completed and complemented the sacrifice of Jesus Christ. Can you say that? Will your death be as the pouring out of wine? Is the wineskin filled with new wine? Life in Jesus can be a meal and a feast.

Paul uses the same word in 2 Timothy 4:6. It is translated here as 'departure', as it is in Philippians 1:23, 'I am ready to depart.' It is used in Luke 12:36, 'When He will return.' There is a suggestion in the Greek word 'Analusis' which gives us all a hope for the future. It means to depart, to go away, to emigrate, to migrate, from winter to warmth, cloud to sunshine. There is no suggestion of the candle being blown out or the life ceasing to exist as in a mist which gathers as the only mourner when we die. It is the word a postman writes on letters when there is no delivery point — *gone away*. Not faded away into oblivion, but gone to a new address, the brass plate outside a shop which stated 'Residence above'.

'Analusis' is a going away to a new area

The word Paul uses 'departure', note, is not death. He is departing from one sphere to enter into another. That which we call dying is just a hill blocking the vision. It is on the horizon, always in front but, when you arrive, it is but a speck of dust, just the mote in the eye, and the finger of Jesus has already written your forgiveness in the dust on the ground.

There are a number of English words which owe their existence to this one Greek word such as *analysis* and *analytical*, that which is placed on either side and analysed until each component is separated from the rest. *Anagram*, the re-formation of a new sentence using each letter to spell out a truth. We will be revised, place in a new body. *Analecta*, small pieces selected from different authors and brought together. All tell of the forming of something new after close examination. It is the opening up, the discovery of what really exists. The only separation you will ever know is the separation of body from soul and spirit and your separation from this world in which you now live.

In Lancashire, England, old houses are knocked down and, along with paving stones are transported to the South of England to be re-erected as beautiful homes and paving for parks. In the old Durham village of Beamish, a whole station has been brought from a different part of the country and re-erected as it used to be. There you can see the past in the present, but we will see the future in the present.

'Analusis' means to be placed in your correct compartment

The word used for dying can suggest the taking of water, dividing it into many parts with each part labelled. It is the splitting of the atom. None is lost in the parting and nothing of you will be lost. Character never dies, personality shall ever be, just as the leaves and the fruit on every tree is but another expression of the life of that tree in stem, root, branch and blossom.

The word 'analusis' is found in the New Testament in 2 Timothy 4:6 with its kindred verb in Philippians 1:23, where it describes the pulling up of the anchor, the slipping of the cable, the moving out to the depths of the open sea. Then in Luke 12:36, it describes returning from a wedding. There is the thought of the return to the original source from whence a person came. We are God's, created by God. We are His workmanship and, from the hand from which the original Adam came, you will return. The Acts of the Apostles states, 'And they being let go, went to their own company.'

In Acts 27:12,13 and 28:10, we have another word from the word 'analusis' — 'anago' — which describes setting the sails and preparing to sail. When you depart this life it is not the lowering of the sails or the flag to half-mast, it is the raising of the sails and the signal to sail away to Paradise Island. There is greater depth, height, length and breadth waiting, for such is the love of God. The whole of Eternity is before you. Death will be the releasing of the ship from the port, the treasure ship. Our destination, your destination, is marked with a cross.

'Analusis' means to go to another place more real than Earth

In John 14:3 Jesus says, 'That where I am, there you may be also. I go to prepare a place for you.' That life which has been has gathered many jewels; character has been developed and all is taken to be used and useful in another realm. This is training for reigning! This is trial and struggle until all the foreign elements are removed and what was iron ore emerges as a new shining pin! This life has been a university, a training for a future use.

The word Paul uses of his death sheds light, and that light appears in the valley of the shadow of death[1]. It is the word of a prisoner, a farmer, a warrior, a seaman, a scientist. One word that is applied to the many areas of life, proving that the best is yet to be, the ending is but a beginning and a going on into something new, not a brick wall but an open door.

'Analusis' is a nautical term

It was a word often used by sailors and sea captains when sailing[2]. It is taken from the vocabulary of the captain of a trading vessel, who feels he has been in foreign ports long enough and now has the desire to depart. The root word means to steer, according to Vincent in *New Testament words*[3]. He wants to get home to his own family, friends and familiar surroundings. The ship has received its sealed orders. It has a full complement. The cargo is fully laden. It is high tide. There is a call from the beyond and, in death, you answer that call.

'Analusis' is a military term

This word was used by the engineers whose work was to reconstruct and to make secure bridges and crossings. With little or no resources they were called upon to design new things from old.

In 2 Corinthians 5:1, the body is seen as a tent, the army ready to 'break camp'. 'Analusis' describes the tent ropes being loosened. The army has heard the call to break camp, to move on into another area. As we die, so there is the loosing of all that has been part of this world. Death is the taking down of the tent for the final time. You have been in the King's Army, have fought a good fight and, as a soldier of Jesus Christ, have endured hardship, but now there is the release from warfare. You are to be demobilised. The Army is going away, breaking camp. Each piece of equipment is placed in its right order, ready to be re-assembled in the future. It has heard a call, the trumpet has sounded. New orders have been received.

'Analusis' is an agricultural term

It was used in ploughing, sowing and reaping and describes, after a hard day's work, the shafts and harness being taken from the animal as it is led into the stable. The day has been long, the furrows many, the chaffing yoke and the rubbing harness are no more. The ploughman takes his beast from the shaft. He has finished his work and is returning to his cottage and family. He is going from the loneliness of the furrow. The work and the sowing has been hard but now he lays it on one side to rest. The burdens on the back of the beast are laid down. There is an unyoking of the yoke. The pain of the blade will be no more. The day has ended.

What the barn, the green grass, the oats and other good foods are to the animals, so the release from the shafts of life will be to you. There will be an entering in to a resting place, the place where plough or cart needs no pulling or straining. The end of the furrow has been reached. The burden has been laid down.

'Analusis' is a philosophical term

It describes a thought which is received yet has been unclear. It is a problem shrouded in mystery which suddenly makes sense. A shaft of light has penetrated the mind. The dawn has come, new light has been received. What has seen through a dark glass, a riddle, an enigma, is seen clearly in a new light. Everything falls into place, into its proper order. Dear reader, trust God. Let Him decide and display all His knowledge in the after life!

The eyes are open wide for us to see things as they really are. In this life we have gazed on most things with cataract vision, stared at heavenly truths with midnight eyes. This word 'analusis' was used in thinking, reasoning and debating at the forum. It described a coming to a conclusion about that which had been a puzzle. It means to solve a problem. The final piece has been placed correctly in the puzzle. Death and the future may seem to be fragmented but there is a mighty hand which will arrange it all.

In 1 Corinthians 15:23 we read 'Every man in his own order.' Every soldier in his own company and rank. The knot has been dissolved, untied. The mathematical problem, the equation has suddenly been worked out, the correct answer given. The dark glass that looked on Eternity and death is dark no more. The problem is solved in death.

All use this word 'analusis'. Every Philosopher — Plato, Homer, Aristotle — looked for the answer to life and death. It was found for you when you were found by Jesus Christ! The grave is not just a mound of earth crowned with flowers. There is a hole in the ground and you will go right through it the moment you arrive at your appointed time.

'Analusis' is an industrial word

This word was used for weaving tapestry and beautiful patterns. It was a working word. It is the fulfilment for you of the word, 'All things work together for good to them that love God.' God has a mosaic of your life, a fair pattern for every life; the design and colours are left to Him.

It was used of weaving, describing the unloosed threads. It was used of Penelope's Web[4], which she wove each day and pulled out each night. It was re-woven each morning and pulled out each night. It is to be taken off the loom, to be re-woven by the hands of Jesus Christ. This weaving will be better than Joseph's coat of many colours. It is body weaving, the new will be as the wine at Cana, the best was last.

'Analusis' is a judicial term

It was written across the pardon received by the prisoner, read aloud on his release; it was the one word which described the loosing of bonds that held the prisoner — loosed, to be judged no more. The sentence was finished, the door wide open into a new life. The sentence is complete. The pardon has been received. Jesus is the key to that which locks up the secrets of the grave. The doors of death spring wide open because of Him.

'Analusis' is a grammatical term

It was used in the schools and universities, the Academies of Greece. All the grammatical components are in correct order. It makes sense. This life has been a jumbled alphabet, we have been as children playing with the A – Z bricks, or as the Toppets, taking a piece from one figure and placing it on another, the end result being like jelly babies, mixed together. Everything will be in its proper place. Every part fitted and functioning in the purpose for which it was designed.

It was used for loosening bonds or fetters. It was used for loosening the ropes of a tent. It was used for the loosening of the moorings of a ship[5]. It was used for the 'departure' of people from one place to a better place. The sense of adventure and voyage was here. It was a voyage to treasure island and to the Eden lost. Such was the word written on the prisoners' pardon, whispered by the captive as he was set free.

'Analusis' means departure to a new world

How different are Paul's words from those of Shakespeare's Hamlet, 'To be or not to be. That is the question.' Death is not just the re-shuffling of the cards for a better hand or the arranging of the flowers in a different vase, it is much more. Life loved, waited for, longed for and dreamed of will be finally entered into.

There is going to be a departure, but there will also be a welcome. We may go silently from this life yet be received as Pilgrim was in Bunyan's *Pilgrim's Progress*, with the blowing of trumpets. Visualise the Roman Caesar returning up the Appian Way in Rome. He is enjoying his triumph. The lost will be found, the unknown will be known, the secret will be made manifest and all will know as they are known. Death for us should hold as little fear as a child fears the love in its mother's eyes.

The reorganisation is left with Him who made the worlds. He made a star to so fit into place that one appears four minutes after the other. He upholds all things by the word of His power and because of Him worlds do not collide but are the best time-pieces in the universe. The sun and moon have their appointed place.

In Heaven there will be no language to learn, no foreign customs for they have been placed within our hearts already by the Spirit of God. We are the colony of Heaven, strangers and foreigners returning to our native land. We are as Jim Hawkins and Captain Livesey returning with a full treasure ship in R. L. Stevenson's *Treasure Island*. No need to be concerned over dress, we are to be arrayed in white linen, the righteousness of the saints, with crowns for the head and the shoes of the returning Prodigal on our feet. We are departing into the dawning of everlasting day, entering into the deep joy of Jesus Christ.

He has everything in hand, even the timetable, the time of our departure. It will be the joy of the just. Freedom from the limits of a body which has weighed upon some of us like a lump of earth. Tiredness, weakness, sickness and pain will be no more. The thorns will be left with the branches. Torn flesh will never be part of the new body. There will be no cancerous growths.

In each one of the pictures the word 'analusis' has presented to us there was life beyond, a new start, a journey home. The struggle and the strains of life are removed. We are grazing, sailing, marching to new frontiers in God.

Are you awaiting your departure, as much as they are awaiting your arrival, in the great Beyond? There is much more awaiting you. There is more...and more...and more....

NOTES

1. There is no mention of death in the original Scriptures of Psalm 23. The word has been added. See author's book, *Paths of Righteousness in Psalm 23*.

2. See Adam Clarke's *New Testament Commentary*; Albert Barnes *Notes on the New Testament*.

3. Vincent on *New Testament Words*, published by Charles Scribners Sons, New York, 1905.

4. Homer's writings, the Greek Philosopher.

5. William Barclay, *Daily Study Bible, 2 Timothy*, page 240.

CHAPTER

4

What Has Happened to
Those in the Cemetery?

When we die, the spirit and the soul pass from the body and the body goes into a hole in the ground, a grave — meaning a ditch. The depth or the size of the grave has no relevance. Collective graves become a cemetery. Abraham commenced this burying of the dead in a cemetery when he bought the plot of land in which to bury Sarah (Genesis 23:3–7). The grave usually, although not exclusively, is in a cemetery. The disciples buried the body of John Baptist (Matthew 14:12).

2 Corinthians 5:1–4 places everything in perspective, speaking of a new body, eternal in the heavens, which will be placed upon us as a new body of a new order. The body that is buried is not the body that shall be. The body in the grave will know corruption, but the corruption must be replaced by incorruption, mortal must put on immortality. This will not be a change of dress, not even a change of style. We must gaze into the grave as a scientist gazes into the night sky. There are more than flowers, there are wreaths of promises. God has placed hope alongside every believer and that hope is never buried in a grave. The smell of death is swallowed up in the scent of new, everlasting life. It is in death that hope has built a castle. In that deep darkness are the seeds of resurrection life.

I am not left alone with my tears and grief, for Jesus has planted seeds of hope which are watered by my tears and soothe my grief. With one small stone, David toppled Goliath of Gath. Jesus, entering the grave or the tomb has toppled the fear of death. The grave need not be a black hole in the ground; the cemetery has no bars or doors. We must view the grave as a door into Heaven, not into the earth. It is a passage, an opening, suggesting there is a leading into something more. Some of God's best blooms are going to spring from here. The grave is as the bedroom, leading into the dawning of a new day. It is in the bedroom that we find the wardrobe. The spirit is going to be 'clothed upon'[1]. Death is but an article used by God. The grave is never the goal, as the cemetery is never the centre of Life after Death. It might be the 'dead centre' of the city, town or village, the place of rest, yet it will become the centre of life, the womb into another world.

There are many suggestions in the words 'grave' and 'cemetery'

One Hebrew word for 'grave' means 'ruin', another means 'destruction'. The grave is seen as a mouth that swallows. It is occasionally referred to as Sheol or Hades, the unseen world. Lamps were left burning with the dead one, to see them through the darkness ahead.

The word cemetery is not in the old King James Version of the Bible, but it is used in the *Berkley Translation in Modern English* in Jeremiah 26:23 to describe the burial places of common people. Graves were sepulchres, tombs and caves, and the surrounding area was the cemetery. Christ walks through each graveyard proclaiming 'I am the Resurrection and the Life. Though he were dead, yet shall he live.' The very dust He used in John 9:6 to anoint the eyes of the blind man He will use to create, not only the seeing eye, but every faculty of the new body. There can only ever be bodily attachments to the grave.

Each grave was supposed to resemble a small bed. God's Acre was the dormitory. Embalming and burial is what happens to remains. The real you steps out of the body the moment you die. Only part is sealed in a tomb. The soul, the spirit, the character is too big to be buried. What you really are is bigger than any mountain, bigger than Mount Everest. It cannot be buried for an hour or a day, certainly not for a thousand years. Whenever we pass from this life it becomes the launch pad into Eternity. It is from here that we arise. If a fish is to get into the depths of the blue ocean it needs a little water, just enough to take it into the depths. Just a little faith in Jesus Christ takes us from the grave and into Eternity. Even if you died in a cemetery you would never remain there! You die in Jesus Christ. Long before the funeral arrangements have been made, faith has accomplished its work. The funeral is the bolting of the door after the horse has escaped!

The Greeks had a word for 'cemetery'

The Greek word for cemetery is 'Koimeterion', from 'Koimao' — I sleep. Where the body is folded as a tent and sleeps sweetly on until it is aroused in another form, all the particles formed into a pattern. The mould is the hand of God. The word cemetery has no thought in it of death. It has that association because of the grave and the dead bodies in the graves. Those in Jesus Christ never die. They sleep the sleep of the just, as a body.

Resting in bed, your body may be asleep whilst your mind is skipping, jumping, rejoicing. There has to be activity while you sleep. There is a whole factory within you at work, renewing, refreshing. The soul does not sleep, the spirit does not take a nap, only the body sleeps[2]. One falls, while the other rises. The soldier falls while the flag flutters in the breeze. When I sleep my spirit, my soul is still living. The ship leaves the cargo in the port and sails on. When sleep is mentioned it refers to the body only. Death was known and referred to as sleep, even by the heathen. (We shall discuss this more fully in the next Chapter.)

The cemetery was used by the first worshippers

The cemetery came from the early gatherings of believers. They were not allowed to own buildings, so occasionally, because of fear, they met outside the cities. As they fellowshipped in the wilderness, in the hills, the place made in a clearing was called a cemetery. The ecclesia (church) met at the kometerion (the cemetery). There was far more life and freedom expressed here than in the city centre. Hearts were tuned to praise and worship, the place people went to hear the Gospel preached. People repented in the burial-ground! It became the place of love, joy, peace, fellowship and mutual understanding. When they referred to the cemetery they were talking about worship, friendship and fellowship — it was a Pentecostal meeting, the place of miracles and the moving of the Spirit of God, the place of grace, the hour of testimony and encouragement, where they broke bread, worshipped and received healing. It was the heart of the early fellowship, they sang and praised the living God, who had said, 'Because I live, you shall live also.'[3]

Later came the thought that it would be a good place to bury the dead, right where they worshipped. Graveyards are yards of graves! To be surrounded by the dead added faith and spice to devotions. Jesus was the sexton of the cemetery. He cared for the sacred vessels buried there, buried in the heart of God, deeper and safer than in a pit of soil.

The cemetery was added to and flowers were introduced

It was later that church buildings were added to the cemetery and hence, churchyards. Churches were built, evolving from the fact that these areas were places of praise and prayer. The flowers were added to the grave later. Each flower laid spoke of eternal life. Flowers were brought which depicted the names of those who had gone into the presence of God — Rose, Lily, Snowdrop, Narcissus, Ivy. They were arranged as dials, each flower opening at a certain time, depicting continuing life.

The word cemetery has the thought in it of sleep, but never death. The Jews referred to death as sleep. The Persians named their cemeteries 'the cities of the silent'. The burial ground was the sleeping place, as the cradle of a child.

The cemetery is where they awaited the trumpet call

The cemetery was a sleeping room, an area of sleeping soldiers and saints. As the Roman soldiers slept they awaited the trumpet call (1 Thessalonians 4:17). 1 Corinthians 15:51,52 says there is going to be a change. This is a changing room. The Greeks thought it was unlucky even to pronounce the word death. They gladly used other terms, terms that were just as empty as the word death but sounded better. 'The repose of the body' sounded better. As the Christians gathered together for worship, the children slept.

The cemetery is an inn or a sleeping place for strangers

It became a stopping off place for the night. Christians used Greek thought in the word 'Koimeterion'. In Greek it described an inn or a lodging house. It was an inn on the way to the sixth happiness. Strangers, pilgrims, travellers, all stayed there. It was just a place to rest in the dark of the night ready to be revived and commence afresh in the light of a new day. In with sackcloth and ashes, out draped in silk, dressed for a new day; the night clothes removed, a day suit worn.

The seed is covered with black soil to appear as a white lily. There are so many shapes and forms in a multiplicity of colours which come from the black soil surrounding us. We bury what we want to keep, just as they buried their treasures in sealed jars, where thief, moth or rust would not break through and steal. Travellers, strangers, stayed at the Koimeterion for safety, rather like our hotels and guest houses.

The cemetery is more than a coffin factory

The cemetery is more than a row of coffins, more than a row of flowers, more than marks made by chisel in marble. It was the place where Jesus met with Mary[4]. He is the Gardener of every cemetery. The best bit of news this world has ever heard came from a graveyard. Jesus first appeared in one when He rose from the dead. In the necropolis of the Christian there are no rich pickings for the undertaker. It is the place of a bed, a person resting, a place to stay until breath is recovered. Being worn out, you rested, staying until the next place was made ready[5]. It is just a bed for the night.

There is only a part of you in God's Acre. That is the best term for the grave. Every body is treasure in a field. The earth is the Lord's and the fullness of it[6]. A little bit of Heaven lies in some foreign field, awaiting the shout, the trumpet call which will bring absent and present together in one final fusion. Those alive or asleep are part of the Colony of Heaven. They are part of God's plan and heart.

As God put Adam to sleep bodily,[7] so each believer is put to sleep and from that sleeping form steps another. God only dealt with one side of Adam. He has to deal with every side of us. The whole body must be dealt with. There will not be a spot or blemish in what God does. Corruption and mortality will be buried, lost forever. Another body came from the sleeping Adam, named Eve, the mother of all living. You will be presented as a chaste virgin, without spot, wrinkle or blemish[8]. From that small pip comes the lovely red apple, from the seed of the fig, the fully-formed fig.

The cemetery contains the goodness and mercy of God

'Surely goodness and mercy shall follow me all the days of my life.'[9] These were as the coachmen accompanying each coach on its journey, going on before and arranging things. Each stopping place was arranged and those travelling in the coach were well catered for. Here the horses were refreshed, new plans were made. The cemetery is the wardrobe, and the bodies will be readjusted, reshaped, reformed, like the glorious body of Jesus Christ. All those buried in its soil will spring forth as lilies of the valley and the rose of Sharon.

Different cemeteries for different beliefs

It was important that, according to belief, the different burial grounds were placed in strategic positions, some with the grave facing east to catch the rising sun, others buried in a standing position to receive the most light and within sight of the city walls, or near the home. Ashes are scattered in many different places. The ancient Chinese had theirs placed where there was running water and plenty of fresh air. Some still have lighted tapers to show the way through death. The Buddhists leave lamps lit and food laid out. There will only be part of you there. The twin side of you will be elsewhere. The lamp and the lampstand will come together in brilliant light.

Strangers could not usually be buried in Jewish cemeteries. The thirty pieces of silver, thrown on the Temple floor by Judas was used to buy a field in which to bury strangers. You might be a stranger to this world, but not to God. There is a place for the believer, purchased by the blood of the Son of God. While Judas was buying a field for strangers, Jesus was purchasing a place for saints, sons, soldiers and servants.

He makes everything special, even death, and your place of the burying of the body. The wrapping paper can be disposed of, as long as we know where the precious content of the parcel is. What the Lord's Day was to the week, so the cemetery was to life. In these burial grounds they held their Love Feasts. The first day of the week was the cemetery.

The cemetery was sanctified by Jesus Christ

Some saw the burial area as a health hazard, but the early Christians never did. They roamed freely, as much at home as in their own house. Each grave was an altar, where the heart and the spirit were absolutely free. It was where neither Roman soldier, moth or rust could creep or break through, to kill and destroy. It was as the meadow to the sheep. The grave was not the end, but the beginning — as a giant footprint walking into Eternity. It was and is where tares could not be sown[10]. Those buried were everlasting memorials. New phrases were written on pieces of wood, formed into the shape of the cross and placed on graves. Written on the sides of caves were 'No longer here!', 'Gone to Jesus', 'Into the Paradise of Peace!', 'Into Eternal Rest!'. It was never like this before Christ.

They tended to meet there, I think, because they expected a resurrection at any moment and wanted to be the first on the scene!

The cemetery tells of a life which has passed into new areas

George was amazed to see his death recorded in the local paper and telephoned to his friend, Harry: 'Did you see that report of my death?' 'Where are you ringing from?' asked Harry!

Martin Luther King, who was assassinated, has these words over his grave: 'Free at last, free at last, thank God Almighty, I am free at last.' Set free, by a bullet! All God's talents will be unearthed. The small and the great will stand before God[11]. You become free to be what you have never been before.

The cemetery will ever be the place of quiet rest

'Koimeterion' entered into the vocabulary of the early Christians because it was used by the Greeks as a term of hospitality, a rest house for strangers, such as Elisha had supplied for him[12]. Where one might change, wash, be rested and dressed, even as Paul's friends provided a lodging for him to spend the night[13]. It was a place reserved for a stranger, a traveller, as the mother of John Mark who had a house in Jerusalem might have had an upper room.

The old *Chambers Dictionary* gives the definition of cemetery as to 'lull to sleep'. The lap of the mother, the child's bed or pram being gently rocked from side to side, a hammock in the soil. The favourite resting place. Teach me to dread the grave as little as my bed. the Koimeterion was part of the hospitality of a nation.

The cemetery was the exchanging of old for new

Two of the early Fathers gave us facts about cemeteries. Eusebius and Tertullian tell us they were used as places of worship. This house, this tabernacle, this earthly occupied flesh shall be destroyed[14]. It shall be dissolved, but we have another in the heavens. With a better quality article there is no problem in disposing of the old broom head. If the handle has broken you are ready for a new one. See and understand how modern inventions have caused you to throw away the old ideas. The old and the new oven; the washing machine; the wireless for the television; gramophone for the compact disc; typewriter exchanged for the computer. For a famous painting you surrender the scribble of a child. The grave is the burying of the handle. The blade will be added at some future date. Some of the different things we didn't understand — until we accepted them. Now, we wonder how we ever managed without them!

The cemetery only houses that which can be destroyed

The contrast here is between what is in the earth and what is in the heavens. A permanent dwelling place. One is cloth, the other stone. Dying is moving out of a tent and into a house, when the winter has arrived.

1 Corinthians 15:36,37 refers to the sowing of a seed, the sowing of acorn which shall be oak, or brown dried seed which shall be beautiful flower. The lowering of the body into its sleeping position is like the sowing of a seed. It is the hand of the farmer, scattering seed into the furrow. Putting a body into a coffin we wrap it in wood. The coffin becomes a pulpit to the fact that all must die. Add to this the fact that Christ is the firstfruit of them that sleep. He has proven it to be fact and not fiction. Genesis 3:19 had been fulfilled. The rest of God's promises will be. The new birth[15] and Pentecost[16], are a fact. There is a final chapter in the Book of God.

The cemetery is the resurrection factory. Once more the carpenter of Nazareth will have His bench, but what lovely articles are to be produced.

The dead body is the wood in stock, the materials ready to be worked on. This is not an artificial limb factory, it is where God will display His finest and final blooms. The cemetery will become the theatre of God, the open air show. God will have an Open Day!

What happened in Acts 16:26, when the earthquake opened all the doors and bands were loosed, will happen again on a grand scale. It was the acquittal, the pardon, the parade of prisoners without chains. It will be the day of absolute acquittal. Death may have seemed to be a prison but it is to be changed. Death is going to be put to death, speared through the heart with life, a shaft of light splitting the darkness into a million minute pieces, unable to be measured on the Richter Scale, the shock waves too much to be recorded. From every grave will be the path of life.

In the early Church the Christians were the flowers, the epitaphs, the words of testimony on the lips of others who were still living. Dying is sleeping, living, resting, then awakening in His likeness. It is letting the body rest on the arms of Jesus. It is seeing the living among the dead. God has no Book of the Dead. His is the Book of Life.

In war, after victory, prisoners and possessions were paraded. The wealth of the war won was displayed. You will be part of what the Romans called a Triumph. Not in chains, not dragged along as reluctant slaves, but adorned with the jewels of grace, with bodies having all faculties, restored in redemption. The full rights of Roman adoption will be yours. The child publicly was given new clothes, the insignia of its new family, the old clothes taken away. The old body will be taken and a new one will be given, publicly. This thing will not be done in a corner.

Abraham Lincoln was asked, 'Are you a Christian?' He buried his face in his hands and wept. then he replied, 'Not until I saw all the graves at Gettysburg.'

Brian attended the funeral of a friend and as the coffin was lowered into the open grave, so faith was lowered into his heart. He suddenly believed in life after death, strangely because of a funeral and all that was said. Everything suddenly made sense, something he could believe in. He became a Christian minister, serving God for many years. He had found the answer to his question, 'Is this all there is to life? A little path leading to the edge of the grave? Is that what life is all about?' Surely not! Surely not! He received Christ that day as the grave received the coffin. It was not the end, but a new beginning. There was for him, and for you, a triumph in death, making the grave the place for the body only while the spirit and the soul moves into another realm, where the reign of God is All in All.

NOTES

1. 2 Corinthians 5:3.
2. 1 Thessalonians 5:23.
3. John 6:39; 11:25,26.
4. John 20:11–17.
5. John 14:1–3.
6. Psalm 24:1.
7. Genesis 2:21.
8. Ephesians 5:27.
9. Psalm 23:6.
10. Matthew 13:25–40.
11. Revelation 13:16; 20:12.
12. 2 Kings 4:10.
13. Acts 28:7; Philemon 22.
14. 2 Corinthians 5:1.
15. John 3:7.
16. Acts 2:1–4.

Somnambulism — Does the Soul Sleep in the Grave?

A t death the body goes to the grave, laid as dust in dust, wrapped in a white shroud and a wooden frame. The soul and the spirit pass from the body into the presence of God[1]. Light goes to light, life goes to life. The spirit belongs to Him. He has a claim and makes a call on that which is within mankind. Those who have served will soar, those in sin will sink. There is no soul sleep. The soul does not sleep, not even for a day or a night. There is the repose of the body, but there is also the resilience of a living spirit which has been brought to life and immortality in Jesus Christ. Let the sleeping sleep because it is night, but those who are of the day go on from the Church terrestrial into the Church celestial.

Some teachers in the early Church taught that those who died had perished, that Jesus had returned to Heaven and there was no future hope. Paul had to write to the believers at Thessalonica, as in 1 Thessalonians 4:13–18, who were being taught and even believed that the resurrection of believers had taken place and they had been left on the corner, waiting for an event that had already happened. They were left with thin air to grasp. The reality of what they believed for had disappeared. Jesus would not be returning.

If that was true then all those who had died had perished, for all had been promised a resurrection. They were to be a part of it with every believer who had shed his body and passed through the veil of death into the world beyond. They had simply been cut adrift, were as floating clouds, or straws blowing in the wind going everywhere, nowhere, somewhere, maybe, one future day. When they had died they had literally gone back to the dust and had simply been added to the particles already making up the ground. From body to ashes and then to dust. It is into this stark background that the Apostle pens the words, 'If this is so, if there is no resurrection, they are of all men most miserable.' They sleep forever in their misery. The mystery of death deepens into darkness and into the sleep of forever. The dead had not only been covered with soil, placed in a hole, but had been covered as with a blanket with the word 'forever'. As it was, so it would be, now and forever.

What about those who sleep in Jesus?

What about those who sleep in Jesus? Have they perished? Are they all Sleeping Beauties or giants laid to rest for ever and a day? These questions were keenly felt by those who trusted in life after death. It was as difficult for these primeval believers to accept as it was for the Israelites to make more bricks out of less straw. Even if they were all asleep, then that was not life after death, it was only breathing, shallow breathing in a shallow grave. There was a firm belief that to be absent from the body was to be present with the Lord, and so is this same writer's argument in 2 Corinthians 5. The God of Israel neither slumbers nor sleeps. The nature of God cannot sleep. That which is implanted at the New Birth into the human spirit[2] cannot slumber or sleep. Eternal life can neither sleep or see corruption[3]. Resting, sleeping, are connected with this life. In the future life there is no night! Sleep is here and now after a hard day's toil, yet the toil has finished for those who have gone before. They have entered, through His rest[4], into their rest. There is no more striving, simply an acceptance of all that has been done through the cross for them. When I come to a rose there is no requirement to manufacture the scent, it is there already, simply to be enjoyed.

The Apostle, along with other writers[5] has to use the term sleep instead of death for those who have died. He cannot refer to them as alive, because that would confuse those receiving and reading his letters with those who are alive in the body.

As stated in the previous chapter, and as you will gather from future chapters of this book, at death there is a parting of body, soul and spirit. They are not literally asleep but bodily they are taking a rest. You can sit down and rest without falling asleep. Your brain, spirit, heartbeat, even thoughts can be very active in a sleeping body. The writers in the New Testament are really saying: 'Think on death as taking a nap. Your plans, your future, all that you are rests with you in your inner nature, in your sparkling spirit until it is set free by death.' That death can be the starter pistol giving the signal to go where you really belong. The believer is of another world, another nature, another side, even as there are two sides to every coin. There are those who would hijack these promises of life continuing after death.

The body goes to the worms, where it belongs, to be changed in a moment in the twinkling of an eye. To be changed as quickly as a wink. The soul and spirit departing into the presence of God, waiting to be clothed upon with a new body — immortality. The essential YOU goes to be with God. It ascends into Abraham's bosom and into Paradise. Two descriptions of the same place of life after death, which you will understand more fully through the future pages of this book. More light will dawn, which the greatest darkness cannot put out.

The body is put to sleep

When the word sleep is mentioned and it is referred to so many times[5], it suggests the sleep of the body which we have seen is placed in the cemetery. It goes into the grave as a body and it may even degenerate into specks of dust. Worms may take it and use it for their crown, yet at the sound of the trumpet that body will be changed. The speck of dust will become a beautiful stone of rarer worth than earth's pockets can afford. The finger of God will again be drawn in that dust. By His power there will be a raising up of a new and glorious body from that which has been inglorious. It will be as the history of the Rose Window in Lincoln Cathedral. Bits of broken coloured glass were scattered around, and an apprentice requested the use of them. He took them, pieced them together and created the Rose Window. God will do that for you on a more glorious scale.

The body does sleep but for you, dear reader, the spirit and the soul ascend to God. It is recorded in the Acts of the Apostles 4:23, 'They being let go went to their own company.' They went to their own. Jesus committed His Spirit into the hands of the Father[6], not to the tomb, and certainly not to soul sleep. In Acts 7:59,60, Stephen, the first Christian martyr committed his spirit into the hands of God, before his body fell asleep until the Resurrection of the dead (verse 60). The hand of death would have clutched at you and bound you but for the death of Jesus

Christ. From death we fly into the presence of God; better still, we are borne there. We can have a sign placed on the grave 'residence above'. The loved one you buried years ago, months ago, days before, is not there.

At the moment of death there is that in the body which passes into the Eternity beyond, to the place Jesus recorded in John 14:1-3, 'I go to prepare a "place" for you.' The word 'place' is where we obtain our English word 'topography' — map drawing, land drawing and arranging. It is a surveyor's word. God is a God of order even in the future unseen world. Hebrews 12:1 sees these departed loved ones as a great cloud of witnesses, beckoning us, seeking to encourage us by their examples. To die in Jesus means to be alive in Him who lives forever. You must first live in Jesus, live for Him, before you can die in Him.

Where do all the leaves, the fruit and the flowers go in the winter? They are inward as sap and bulb, not dead, not even asleep, but awaiting the call of Spring. Tree, leaf, fruit, bulb, stem and flower will come together to have a glorious party in the summer sun. The steam in the steam engine, electricity in the electric engine move into the wheel as power is released. While the engine is stationary, that power is still there. It is neither switched off, nor dead.

When the winter of death comes, it need not be your winter of discontent. We go to the bright burning fireside of God's unchanging love. Those who are the Lord's are the Lord's forever. They are marked with a sign. This theme, that there is no perishing, no sleeping, no wasting or casting away at death runs right through the New Testament. It is mentioned some 280 times and it is spoken of more than hell or Heaven. It is there to present you with a bouquet of assurance, to fill the valley of death with the streaming light of a dawning new day. You can rest without being asleep and your body can be asleep while that which is within you is very much alive. You have sweet dreams while sleeping. There may be the pronouncement of being clinically dead, and yet the discovery has been made on a number of occasions that the person was very much alive.

Jesus said, 'Come unto me all you who are weary and heavy laden and I will give you rest.' He did not say, Come and I will send you into a deep sleep for a million years. The Book of Revelation represents those souls who have died, crying, praying and asking, but who are under the Throne of God proving that they live on and are more wide awake than ever[7]. The eyes might be closed at death but they are opened to something far greater than that seen by the eyes of the body. The body might hibernate while the spirit is free to travel through every forest glade. That which has been limited as a body with aches and pains, hurts and bruises is released from the chains which bound it in bodily shape, into the presence of God. It waits there as a sentry asleep to receive a new, everlasting body with resurrection qualities.

Jesus is proof that we do not sleep after death

1 Corinthians 15:19,20 says Jesus is the firstfruits of them that slept. He is alive after death and because He lives, we shall live also. Thirteen resurrection appearances prove that He is still very much alive and all who die do so in Him. He did not lie in the grave to be made better after being wounded on the cross. He went to the grave to produce and to provide evidence for us who are alive, to prove that as we reach for the nettle we might find it has no sting. Death is the awakening of man to the reality of the Eternity which beckons into life with all its fullness.

If a soul went to sleep at death until Jesus came again there would be a vacuum in the promises of God. There would be a part of life unaccounted for. Personal history would be cut off at the grave. There would be an unconsciousness of God and His love, and that can never be. You do not die and live in God to become an island in a sea, or one shell on a beach. This day will you be in Paradise with me! There will never be even the width of the grave or coffin between the believer and his Christ. Paul says, Those who have departed God will bring with Him. They have constantly been at His side, like the angels who always behold the face of the Father. The loving kindness and tender mercies of God do not stop with the hearse, they are not buried in the grave. His love is before, beyond and underneath the grave. That love is the rainbow on which we ascend into His Presence.

We do not cease to be active after death

Even while a person sleeps physically, they do not cease to exist. While the body is in the grave we do not cease to be. You are more than clay, more than body. There is a spirit within you yearning to be released at death to go to your proper place. Whilst on earth you have been but a stranger and a sojourner. Death is not only going home, it is getting home. It is as the fish thrown into the deep sea where it really belongs, after being in the keepnet. You may arrive there without your overcoat, your body, but you will be allowed in. Whether we live or die, we are the Lord's. It is home from home for you, your summer residence in God.

The word used for sleep (Greek *Katheudo*) in the New Testament means to lay down. The opposite word is resurrection (Greek *Anastasis*), meaning to stand up, to stand out. The body is laid down as old and worn, dead and buried. The call of the inner man is upward, onward, forward into all that is God. The immensity of God awaits the immensity of your spirit. All that you were designed to be you are going to be. Everything will fall into place. Everything in its own order, its own ranks. If you, dear reader, belong to God, you have a whole new life, a new order, a new dimension in which you can be neither knocked down or knocked out. Unlike the flame of a candle it cannot be blown out, nor can it be switched off as with an electric light. It is light in the Lord, life in the Lord, the continuation of another form of life in another world.

The Bible speaks of many who are dead yet are alive in another context. 1 Thessalonians 5:6 says there are those who are alive but are asleep to God and His gospel, knowing nothing of the power of God. They judge everything by sight, touch, smell and tradition, alive in their bodies but asleep in spirit. At death the reversal is the truth. Asleep in the body, but very much alive in God in the spirit. The spirit is as wide awake as the open eye refreshed by sleep. Every spirit is a dawn, not a dusk. In Luke 15, the Prodigal Son was alive but it says 'he came to himself'. The dead can be thought upon as being dead, yet they are very much alive, in fact more alive than ever they were in a human body. They die with the words on their lips, 'Free to be what I have always wanted to be.' Dead to us, asleep to us, yet alive because absent from the body is to be present with God, at home with God, signifying to be with one's own people[8]. As long as Eternity is, so the spirit is alive in that same immensity.

Part of you is from Adam, the dust, the red earth. The other part is of God. God breathed into Adam the breath of life[9]. There must have been a moment in the annals of Adam when, as a body, he existed before God breathed spirit into him. Where was that spirit before he became a living soul? That which is of God and from God has not slept a wink in a million years. There never was one yawn attributed to the life of God. The life beyond is a life of new dimensions. Just as life here and now can be joy unspeakable and full of glory, so is life after death for the faithful. Here, the flower is growing. In Eternity it reaches its full potential. Without death we would never reach the full maturity that God intended for us. Death is another sword or dagger blade (made blunt and acceptable, almost turned into a ceremonial sword) for shaping for the future. Through it we are knighted and arise part of a new order.

Nothing can separate you from the love and life of God

Romans 8:35–39 says not even death can separate you from the love of God. The coffin presents no barriers to God. Psalm 23, 'You are with me,' should just read, 'You — me.' Not even a comma in between. A spade full of soil will never come between you and your God. The filling in of the grave will never blot out the light, the supreme light of God's presence.

The gravedigger was asked, 'Are you permanent, here?' 'No,' he replied, 'I am just filling in!'

It is the same with our bodies. That which is the real you has departed as a dove in flight to another branch. As it moves in flight and disappears it dies to that particular area and scene but in the new sphere it is very much alive. It may leave some feathers behind as evidence of a former presence.

Romans 13:11 describes those who are asleep to the gospel message yet, in reality, they are very much alive and well. Those who have passed on are dead, they are asleep as far as we are concerned, but they are neither dead nor asleep to the future world into which they have gone. There is a sense in which everything in the sea is asleep to those on the land. We have to take the plunge to discover its unseen world. Those who have gone before have no body limitations to restrict, no feeble knees which need strengthening, no hands which need lifting up. The body is simply the residence of the soul and the spirit, just as the castle is the residence of the king. They are free at last and it is a lasting freedom. They did not breathe out their last, they breathed in their first! It is the bursting forth of a child being born. It was not into the darkness of night but into the dawning of the day. Alive and well on the hills of God.

The heathen belief in soul sleep

The heathen always referred to those who had died as being asleep. The writers in the New Testament could not simply refer to departed loved ones as having died. Even the heathen did not believe that those who passed on had died, rather they said they were asleep. That word is used but added to it is 'in Jesus'. They sleep not in the earth, not in the memory, not in the images of the mind, but in Jesus Christ. The true nature and destination of the trusting triumphant is that in Him we live and move and have our being, not in a coffin, but in Christ.

It is here that the river never runs dry. The life of God is an everlasting life. God grows neither weary nor tired. He does not have to go to sleep. Why do some say that the Eternal life we received when we repented and believed in Jesus needs to take a nap? This sleeping process, apart from the body, is contrary to the nature of God. The dead do not lay down wearily to rest their spirits. They have no requirement to do so. The wearying part of this life, the body you have, has been laid off as a robe. You have finished with that body, it has served its full purpose and you are free. The guard may sleep, but the soldiers will fight on!

There is excitement and activity after death

How can they be asleep with such exciting things happening around them? Abraham's bosom, Paradise, celestial city, streets of gold, angelic choirs, all are part of their future. So much to tell, so much to see, so great a God to worship.

There was a day when the local florist mixed up his order form information. Two bunches of flowers were ordered, one for a family in grief, the other to a firm which had opened a new office block. The one sent to the grieving family read, 'Congratulations on your new location!' This is the message of life after death.

The fishing smack having unloaded its catch is waiting in the shallow waters, yet it has not sunk, it is not finished with. The fisherman working the ship has stepped on shore, away from the choppy seas. He is very much alive! He has family and friends. Sometimes the nets are being repaired or a new coat of paint is being stretched across. There is no suggestion of death or sleep, it is just in another area with other activities taking place. Sometimes we seek to express the realities of Heaven in the crude caricatures of earth's language and are so clumsy. Everything will be better, more full, deeper, brighter than I can ever say through the pages of this cold print. It is more round than the curve of my mind. The largeness of the expansion is more than the elasticity of that mind. How can my mind, your mind, give expression to the celestial?

Proverbs 4:12 in a free translation says: 'When you go, the way shall be opened up before you step by step.' The saintly Rutherford once said, 'No matter how matters go, the worst will be a tired traveller and a joyful sweet welcome home.' Here is where you really long to be. It is not a house with bricks and mortar, four walls and three doors, windows and curtains, a semi or a two up and two down; it will be all up. There will be no concrete path coming to the front door. It is an atmosphere where the spirits of just men have been made perfect.

Jesus Christ did not sleep in death

Jeremy Taylor said, 'As the soul of Christ after His death did exercise acts of life and grace, it did not sleep.' He visited spirits in prison and preached unto them[10]. From this we may conclude that the souls of the departed are alive and well and are engaged in acts of life.

Paul was caught up into the third Heaven[11], and was very much alive, so alive that he heard unutterable things. Your ultimate destiny is not an out of the body experience, it is out of this earthly tabernacle which will be dissolved. We might be away from our own people, but we are never away from God.

The tree in winter, as the snow in summer, is not dead or asleep, just held in reserve for the correct conditions, where there can be a fuller expression of capacity and capability.

There are evidences of being awake and active after death

Luke 16 is a picture drawn in human minds about the state of life after death by Jesus Christ. Here is the academy of life after death. Experts will try to suggest it is only a parable. A parable of what? Life after death, like the parable of the Prodigal Son was just a parable of the soul away from God? If it is just a parable, then this earthly story must convey some Heavenly truth. There are those throughout the Old and New Testaments who are seen alive and well after death. The apple, pear, lemon or even a cherry hanging from the branch of the tree is the sap of the tree in a body. Within the tree the sap is there. That body, that lemon, is sap in another shape and size.

Here, as Lazarus is out of the body, all the feelings and facts of life are attributed to him after death. He is not asleep. Sleep is never mentioned. He is conveyed by angels. He can remember, see, touch, taste, speak, look and listen. Everything we have now we will have when we have departed from the body. There is a certain freedom which we do not possess now but we will possess it then.

In spite of what has been poetically written, the dead are not the sparkle in the stars or the rush of the upward wind. They are not the fresh breath of a baby or part of the new dawn, nor are they the glitter in the precious stone. They are with God, who works all things after the pleasure of His own good will. Stars may fall, precious stones may be shattered, the fresh breeze can blow no more, but God is forever and ever. Safer than a Yale lock or a clasped hand is the presence of God. The most secure part of each one dying is with the most secure Person in the universe. The iron, the steel, the granite, the strength of His character has become their charter for Eternity.

NOTES

1. 2 Corinthians 5:8,9; Ecclesiastes 12:7.
2. John 3:7.
3. 1 Peter 1:23; 3:4; 1 Corinthians 15:50.
4. Hebrews 4:9,11.
5. Matthew 9:24; 27:52; John 11:11; 1 Corinthians 11:30.
6. Luke 23:46.
7. Revelation 6:9; 20:4.
8. 2 Corinthians 5:8.
9. Genesis 2:7.
10. 1 Peter 3:19.
11. 2 Corinthians 12:2.

CHAPTER
6

Is There Another Existence Beyond the Grave?

Maybe you have thought that the word 'deceased' meant that those who died ceased to exist. Many words do not actually mean the way that they sound. Many old words now have new meanings that were never a part of what they first really meant. There is a tendency, as the years go by, to paint them with new paint. The word decease comes from the New Testament. Peter is the aged servant, the old man of the Church, ready for death and dying. He describes what is about to happen to him as a putting off of a tabernacle for a more permanent dwelling. It is not the end. It is a putting off to put on. Off with the suit he has worn and into new attire. He writes of his decease in 2 Peter 1:13–15. Twice the body is called a tent, which can be put up or taken down. When Israel marched out of Egypt they took the Tabernacle down as a sign that they were going into a new area. Peter uses the word 'decease' once, and it is the twin of Paul's word 'departure'[1]. It means to take down the tent and to erect it elsewhere. If the tent is folded and left, the occupant simply moves on to something better.

In John 1:14, the body of Jesus is described as a tent, describing Him as 'dwelling' amongst us, or tabernacling with us. To Cephas, the aged, the promises of God are as tent pegs, his life as a constant journey. There will be a future and a path to tread. Goodness and mercy shall follow you all the days of your forever life[2]. The goodness of God will see you and yours into the land of the living. Mercy will open your eyes to see wondrous things.

There are new areas, new battlefields, new vistas awaiting Peter. That journey, that structure and mode of abode will be required no longer. Strangers and pilgrims will become sons and daughters, not just passing through as a cloud of dust but naturalised citizens, permanent dwellers in a city which has foundations. The Great Shepherd of the sheep will fold up the tent. Out on the hillsides no longer it will not be required. Paul, the tent-maker, has become a house builder, a temple builder with foundations, which is a picture of the eternal body and state that you will enter into through Jesus Christ. There is an in-between period, an awaiting of the resurrection, but Peter is ready to put off the old worn-out body and is looking forward to something new in God. An excitement of pleasure without measure awaits all who go into the heavenlies and the presence of God.

There will be a travelling on after death

It is thought that the figure used here of death is taken from the Patriarchs as they travelled and had no continuing city. In 2 Corinthians 5:1–10, Paul the Apostle expresses the same tent truth. Here we have the immortal soul in a mortal body, just as the Tabernacle housed the glory of God. He sees himself leaving the tent and, with his work completed, he is going to the better body. There has to be a path from the tent into the presence of God. The tent will be surplus to requirements, when something more secure is seen. The booths in which Israel dwelt when they came to Jerusalem to worship will be of little use. The sock is taken from the foot, the glove from the hand. Neither action suggests sleep or the extinction of any faculty, let alone the body. The New Testament truth is the reversal of soul sleep. We are asleep in a measure now. Death is the true awakening to Eternal realities and richness. When we die we put off this garment, this body of flesh and sleep.

While in the body here Peter sees himself as living in a tent. He is away from home, yet has the reality of being alive and fully conscious of the Eternal world. Then he will move into the permanent abode. O death, where is your victory? Sleep would proclaim death to be victorious. There is no anaesthetic in this dying, only analusis — departing to depart no more. There is a glorious contrast between Judas and Peter or Paul at death. Judas went out, it was night, and he hanged himself. He died uttering the words, 'I have betrayed innocent blood.' Peter unites the thought of the tent and the Exodus. Tradition says that Peter was crucified upside down refusing to be crucified in the same position as his Lord. This, some seem to think, fulfilled the words of Jesus to him[3].

There will be an exodus

The same word 'decease' is used of Jesus in Luke 9:31. They talked with Him of His exodus. 'Decease', our English word, is from the Latin 'decessus', a going away. Don't get your roots too firm, for you are going away! Don't build too much or get too wrapped up in this world, for you are going away. Get your baggage together! Israel in Egypt, after the signs and wonders, were waiting for a word from Moses. Peter is basing his belief on the decease of Jesus. In Luke 9:31, they talked of victory and accomplishment.

In Philippians 1:23, Paul uses another word for death, 'depart'. Luke mentions it again in Acts 20:29. He is describing in nautical terms the loosing of an anchor. It is the removing of the bandage from hurt eyes which have been blind but now are healed. In 2 Timothy 4:6 the word 'departure' means that which is analysed — when a body is taken apart. When you die, body, soul and spirit are divided. This is a forensic word. Each part to its own department. During a post mortem every part is detached and analysed, weighed and marked. The analytic describes a taking apart and a placing under different headings. The body to the grave, the soul to God.

The same word 'analusis' describes the oxen being unyoked from the plough. The cart and the plough have returned to its place of keeping. The oxen is free to roam in pastures of tender grass. There is no thought of death or sleep here. Away into the stud farm or into the greenest of pastures to know the tranquility of total trust. The future is opening as a gate into a large field. The presence of God is something larger and better than anything known in this life. What is flickering firelight compared with a bright sunny day?[4]

We know that God is a Spirit, yet all the attributes of the body are given to Him who has no body. We speak of the mouth of God, the finger of God, the arm of God, the feet of God. In Spirit form, yet He has all these faculties. If that same Spirit, that same life dwells in us through Adam and is then renewed in Jesus Christ, shall we be less than what God is as a Spirit? The answer is No. In the intermediate stage, there will be happenings and functions which we would readily relate to a body.

There is future excitement and fulfilment

When I was a youngster, along with friends, we delighted to help with the release of the 'pit ponies' every summer holiday. the ponies had worked hard all the year, some in deep mines and difficult conditions of water, pulling steel tubs, girders and props, very often in danger. When they were brought up from the mine, once they smelled the open air and the green fields they would move very swiftly, taking on new life and vigour.

You will feel like that as you pass into Eternity. Up from the dark experiences of life, the cruelties of the climate, and into new pastures, into fresh air, where the blooms of God grow perenially. Out of darkness into His most marvellous light. Away from seeing through a glass darkly, and into perfect vision, seeing all, knowing all, enriched by it all in the presence of Him who is defined and demonstrated as the All in All. Into the fullness of knowing, where all doubts are converted into certainties, to the place where the morning of the mind sees everything in bright morning light. The questioning, the desiring, all blown away as cobwebs by His presence.

There are contrasting places after death

Judas, Acts 1:25, went to his own place, which can describe a farm cottage. The bed and breakfast in exchange for the banquet. The small place, the empty place, the place of the faded rose and the blighted memory, where desire and designs, agonies and accomplishments lay as tools with broken shafts. There are those who go to their own place and there are those who go to God's place. One of the first questions the disciples ever asked Jesus was, 'Where do You live?' They went to stay with Him for a full day. A day of Heaven on earth[5]. On the Emmaus Road they asked Him to abide with them for it was towards evening[6].

There is a choice. Judas provided his own eternal lodging, while Jesus takes the place and immediately fills it with many mansions. There is nothing barren about Heaven. John 14:1,2 says it is a place. It is where you can place an object, a table, a chair. There is a place for all in the room. 'I go to prepare a place' (Greek *topes* from where we get the word topography, meaning land contour and map drawing). The word topic comes from this same word. Heaven is our topic. God is our topic. It does not yet appear what we shall be, because we look heavenward through a broken telescope. We have thought on the after life as one looking at the stars through the glass of a common window. When that glass is changed and it magnifies everything a million times we realise there is so much more than we understood. With human eyes we see darkly through a glass, yet there are specifics about life after death, as Peter is stating. There are things we can and do know.

There will never be a leap into the darkness

It is not a leap into the dark but a walking on in the light. The light of what you believe, have received and know will shine the brightest on the day of your disappearing. It will be a walk in the park. 'Today you will be with me in Paradise.' There is no darkness, not even a shadow. Every promise made is a shaft of light. You will have no recognition of going to sleep. Your appointment is neither with death, darkness or sleep, but is an appreciation of being wide awake. The full eye, the bubble and the bounding of life will always be yours, both now, then and forevermore. It may be as entering a dark tunnel, but the Light of Jesus Christ is within. It is a walk with God, as Enoch walked with God and was not, for God took him. He pleased God, and God pleased him. They were a pleasure to each other.

At death you enter into perfection, the perfection of the life of God. There is no weariness or flaw in that nature. Sleep is part of the imperfect life. Life after death is a fullness maintained, never needing to be topped up. The youthful part is part of the after life. All the vigour and virtue is here and now. We have an imperfect body and mind which require sleep for renewal. Sleep is the hand of the sower sowing back into the body what the day has harvested. There will be no requirement for the imperfection of sleep.

Hebrews 11:22 says Joseph believed in a resurrection and in a promised land of the future. He committed his bones to the Exodus. Both Moses and Elijah appeared after death as normal people.[7] Not asleep but wider awake than they had ever been. They were part of a fearless fellowship of friends.

With Peter there is no suggestion of cessation. It is not a brick wall or a hole in the ground but a way ahead. The very word used for decease is the Hebrew word 'exodus' meaning a WAY OUT, a way through, a way up and a way in. Decease never means decrease. It never means death. It is a putting off. It is not the promise of something less but something more. When the Israelites went out in the Exodus, God led them by the right way.

We often refer to the deceased as if they are no more. The seed sown or the plant planted, to use the metaphor of the Apostle Paul in 1 Corinthians 15, has a way out. Sown in weakness and even dishonour it will finally be raised as something glorious. Just as that dried seed or dirty bulb is changed by planting, so will you be. First, you have to leave the body that you now have. There is but a little walk from the prison to the palace. God has sent His Son to walk with you, to direct you.

There will always be difficulties when describing future life

Sometimes, although we have true facts about Heaven, we are like the two children who stood with their little blind friend before a shop window filled with Christmas toys, trying to explain how they looked, the colours, sizes and shapes. They did a woeful job when it came to a full explanation to a small mind and blind eyes. Little wonder that the blind child kept scratching its head as they were speaking. We are as that blind child until we see face to face, and are known as we are known.

If I ask you to close your eyes and think of a house I wonder what enters your mind? Different people will see different houses. Some in rows, semis, detached, and so on. If I give you certain suggestions before asking you to think, it will make all the difference to the way you visualise a house. If I say it has gates with a wall around it, with guards on the gate, a flag fluttering in the breeze and if I added that the Queen lives there, what a difference that would make to what you would see in your mind. It is like that sometimes when describing life after death. We are trying to describe beautiful things in sounding brass and tinkling silver, trying to carve in ice and water. It is almost like trying to describe frozen rivers to those who have never experienced snow or ice. There is the feeling, when expounding the future, of trying to form a knot out of a rope of sand, yet the facts are there. Many people have said to me, 'Where do you get all those facts from of life after death?' The answer my friend is not blowing in the wind but taken from the Word of God. It is a mirror and, if you look into it, you will see pictures of life after death.

In Luke 9:30 the same word 'decease' is used of the death of Jesus Christ who arose from the dead. As Israel journeyed from Egypt to Canaan so there is a way through. The cloud plotted the stages and arranged the stops and starts. The Red Sea, and the River Jordan have been dealt with by Jesus Christ who went forth as Joshua with a spear in his hand. He has made a way out and a way in for us. There is a way through death that suggests less than an end, more than finality.

There is the exegesis of existence in exodus

Certain words beginning with 'ex' have the meaning of abundance that is not the end, not even the beginning, but more and more. Words such as excelling, exit, extreme, extra, exciting, explosion. Extreme means beyond measure. It is not the end of the march, it is only the beginning. Israel went out with the noise of trumpets. Moses and Aaron went up a mountain, to be seen no more.

The English word for decease simply means to go away. Flying as an aeroplane granted a flight path, to a destination. It is not just an opening door or a pathway leading nowhere, it is an open road. There is the thought of the immigrant. The first holiday! Do you remember it? The little child who saw the sea for the first time and ran off the bus to get to it before it disappeared! Here was something there was enough of! A child from an orphanage kissed the bus on which he had travelled for a day's outing. Exciting things will replace the clouds, kisses will be as the sunshine in all its strength.

Death is neither a building without windows or doors or a barn in the middle of a corn field where there are no roads or paths leading from it. The best way leading through death is the way that Jesus Christ went. There are great footsteps through it, left by Jesus. He has sanctified it by His presence. He fills it with His presence just as He fills pain and suffering. We are following Him as Peter followed Him, but not afar. 'I go before my sheep. I go before you into Galilee.' Jesus Himself drew near to those on the Emmaus Road and went with them. Jesus, in the Book of Hebrews, is referred to as the 'pioneer', the forerunner[8]. The forerunner, the pioneer, describes the Macedonian elite force who acted as commandoes going before the main party, rather like Indian scouts preparing the way for the rest of the party. Just as John Baptist did for Jesus Christ[9].

There is a way through and out of death

The decease is the WAY OUT, the Exodus. The forty years of wandering will happen in a moment of time for you. On earth one moment, into the bliss of the presence of God the next. It could happen before you finish reading this book! The Exodus will not take a multiplication of words or chapters, it will take but one word and one happening. One word, 'Exodus' fills a book in the Bible with the many happenings and miracles which took place as they passed out of Egypt. It is made up of thirty-seven chapters and covers a time space of forty years. I have another journey to take, Peter is saying, to make you pure on earth I want to talk to you about Heaven.

Lazarus, in the Gospel of Luke, after death, had all the qualities which matters: name, place, position. Jesus knew where he was. Each one He raised from the dead He knew where they were. He called them back into this life. When you die, the order of being called back from the dead is reversed. You are called into death, unto the side of Jesus Christ. The chief end of man is to glorify God and to enjoy Him forever.

There will be ample provision in and through death

There will be no Red Sea to part or Jordan to stand still. It has already been done. There will be no smiting of the waters of Jordan as Elijah did. It was during this Exodus that judgement fell on Dathan and Korah. There will be no thirsting, as at Meribah, no tempting of God. Manna will not fall from the skies, quails will not be needed. There will be no smitten rock, only a Christ with scars on His hands, feet, side and head. Not Mount Sinai, but Zion, the Heavenly City. The prostitute becomes a Bride in God. The real Manna will be Jesus. We shall be led from fountain to fountain of pure water springing up. Unlike all other religions there will be no requirement to place water, food or finance, not even a light by the side of the dead corpse. The rod will have been removed. There will be the easy tread on streets of gold.

The wilderness was sparsely populated and its herbage small, but there are palm trees and fruit trees. The tambourine of Miriam is replaced by harps of gold. Spies become saints. There will be no Sabbath Day to break by the gathering of sticks. It will be a perpetual Sabbath. The sky will not be dark, requiring a pillar of fire or white cloud. There will be no night there, no serpents to bite, no healing will be required. Every man will be a physician within himself. His hands will administer glory wherever he goes. There will be no rebellion. All will be in subjection to the Lord's Christ. We shall not be seeking the way, we shall be on the way, with no corners, bends or horizons. There will be no death. They who sat in the region and shadow of death, for them light has sprung up. We will have no foreign tribes to face, every man will be a brother and every woman a sister, as one in Christ. No marriage, but as the angels of God. Married as a bride to Jesus Christ.

The Battles of Rephadim and other wars will be ended. There are no walls of Jericho to fall flat, or Ai to take after defeat. All has been accomplished on this Exodus. Think of Israel leaving the flesh pots of Egypt. Everything was accomplished for them before they commenced. God prepared a table in the wilderness, their bread and water was sure.

There will be a marching out, a going on

Exodus: Jerome called it the 'Out going, marching out'. Final, complete, wholesale. They left nothing behind in Egypt, not even Joseph's body. They went out full, not one lame person amongst them. Their clothes never wore out. What a manner of blessing will you take with you? What contribution will you make to Heaven? Will you be as a diamond, an amethyst, carbuncle, opal? Your character, your worth can be like one of these precious stones. What shall I give for you? What shall I compare you to? Heaven will never be the perfection it is without you. It would be incomplete. One of the sheep would be missing. The heart of God would not rest easy. There will not be one stitch left as we enter our Exodus. It will be a march on as we shall discover in the words Paul uses to describe death.

While at home in this tent, we have been absent from the real residence of God. Every place in Heaven is near to the throne. Every person sees His glory. In this life you have been on the inside looking out. The day is coming when you will be on the outside looking in and up, as free as the kite in the wind or the bird in the air. After gazing for years from the prison window, longing for the other side of the doors, those doors at death will be opened wide, wide enough for all that is really you to pass through as the Exodus takes place. The sights and sounds you have only imagined, simply reflected in a mirror, will become the whole symphony.

We have heard reports and seen in paintings the clumsy scratchings of the artist, listened to descriptions in words, falling as pebbles onto the concrete path. What is the artist's impression of a clear sky when compared with the reality? As the hymn says, 'with unbeclouded eyes' we shall see, know and face the facts for themselves. The best wine will be kept until the last. The last drop is better and sweeter than all the tastes of this earth. What we have and know now, our highest delights and tranquil moments are but brackish and mute when compared with that which is before us.

Be encouraged as the marching nation was as they shouted Exodus! Exodus! Exodus! to one another. We are going out today. What has been given in secret and has been very much a mystery is going to be shown openly. The disciples said, 'Tell us plainly that You are the Christ.' He will tell it so plainly that the mute mind would fully understand, the deaf ear will hear, the blind eye will see, the broken leg will leap because of it! The wish, the desire, is going to be the promise fulfilled, the thought translated into the deed.

He who said, I will arise from the dead, also said, I will come again. I pray that you might be where I am[10]. I will receive you unto myself. Everything He said was fulfilled, as your promises of life after death will be. He has signed the article of life after death in His own blood and with a nail from His cross. That which is soaked in blood must be fully accomplished.

There will be eternal acceptance in the beloved

Finally accepted in the Beloved. That same word 'accepted' is the word used of Mary: You are 'highly favoured'[11]. From the unknown into the known, from the dark and the dank into your Eternal habitation. 'I will be their God and they shall be my people.'

I was raised in a small mining village in a terraced house. The door fell off its hinges, the roof caved in, the windows would not open and the floor boards were rotting. We had rats and cockroaches. We were so excited when we were allocated a new house. What a contrast between the old dwelling and the new, so much to discover. The boredom of the old condemned house was forgotten in the splendid garden and the new rooms. Everything in this house was electric. In the former dwelling it had been coal fire and paraffin. This was a life and a dwelling of a new order, as different as gas and electric from oil and paraffin. We were children, we could not provide this, it was provided for us by others and we simply entered into it. It opened up a whole new world, a new life. The new life in Jesus will be displayed in a million forms of life. Every human being is different, and so is every part of the after life. It is here that individuality will be seen collectively.

As the Christian was dying the question was asked, Who are you? The reply was, looking back, sorrow and remorse, but looking forward I am joy unspeakable and full of glory!

'How are you?' one dying saint was asked. 'I am just packing up, ready to be off,' was the reply.

The only thing you take with you from this life is Jesus Christ, and all things relative to the Kingdom of God. You will be as acceptable as food to an open mouth and hungry stomach, as acceptable as light is to the eye.

May God bring you into that anticipation of your own exodus. It will be 'goodbye', but it will also be 'welcome' on the other side. My mother had a mat and on one side it said 'Welcome', on the other it said 'Goodbye'.

It is a leaving of this life and an exodus into a new life of immeasurable expansion. Decease is not what I thought it was. It is not what I was taught. It is something far more. It is all you have and all you are. All you have allowed God to make you. Finding a true role and fulfilment after being a fragment, finding all fullness in the fullness and immensity of God, who fills all things, and fills Eternity.

NOTES

1. 2 Timothy 4:6.

2. See author's book, *Paths of Righteousness in Psalm 23*.

3. John 21:18.

4. We shall discuss this more fully in the next chapter.

5. John 1:37–39.

6. Luke 24:29.
7. Luke 9:30.
8. Hebrews 6:20.
9. Matthew 3:3.
10. John 14:3; 17:24.
11. Luke 1:28.

CHAPTER

7

What Does 'Being in Paradise' Mean?

Through the chapters of this book we now come to recognising some of the things around us and tasting some of the pleasures that are being prepared. Abraham's bosom presents one aspect of life after death, that of a rare position, while another aspect brings into focus a rare place of provision. There are things surrounding us which we need to note, things which eye has never seen, lips never tasted, or the ear heard await those who love the thought of His appearing. It is part of that which has been prepared for them that love Him[1]. Yet it is not the whole.

Paradise defined as a dormitory

H. G. Wells used to say, 'The difficulty of writing about another world in our language is almost an impossibility!' Another language, another vocabulary is required. It is sometimes beyond the curve of the mind. We can, however, describe what Jesus said about life and death. We can give the background history, add colour and contour into words which, by constant use, have lost meaning and appeal. Paradise is such a word.

As the time approaches to pass into the shoreless zone of Eternity, there is no time of suffering to atone for sins when death finally calls and displays its throne. There is a new King on that throne, called Jesus Christ, the Conqueror of Death and of Hades[2]. It will be earth and Paradise today, not tomorrow. Absent from the body, present with the Lord. Paradise has plants of glory planted from the seeds sown by Christ, deeply rooted in His righteousness and death on the Cross.

Paradise is defined as the abode of the saints of God. It is the waiting room, the ambience of a great King. It is part of the harem with all its flowing spices as the maidens prepared to meet the King in all his glory. It is described as the side palace of Eglon's garden in the Old Testament[3].

Paradise is the pleasurable aspect of Eternity when all that was promised will be realised by the believer. Here is your Gold Coast, your rest after an eventful life and death, part of the Will and Testament of Jesus Christ. He is alive to see every crossing of the *T* and dotting of the *I*. Paradise, pearly gates, streets of gold, peoples of every tribe, tongue and nation, praising and playing harps, are all part of the final destination — Heaven. In the meanwhile, before the dramatic Greek play we have a lesser happening found expressed fully in the word Paradise.

Paradise is a delightsome land

The words of the famous hymn will be answered and completed:

'Nearer, my God to Thee.'

Thou, you and me, shall be in Paradise today; future bliss. This is what Christianity is all about. We shall go to that which has been prepared, discovered and uncovered in Jesus Christ.

Browning wrote the famous lines, 'Oh to be in England, now that April's here' — yet it is better to be in the Paradise of God! Life here might have been ploughing and sowing but Paradise will bring that reaping, in fact a golden harvest. The clay you have been using in this life has contained much gravel but there are easier times ahead. The dark tunnel will burst its sides through the power of light in Paradise. There will be a resting in silk.

What and where is Paradise? What do the flowers of Paradise mean? What does Paradise suggest? Where did the dying thief go? What was Jesus suggesting about life after death? He did not want to paint a strong delusion, or allow us to be lowered onto a lie as we die. This promise of Paradise is as the rose which grows at the side of the rusty rails. It is not a case of pie in the sky, but hope in the heart from the start. It is the knowledge and assurance given by the Holy Spirit of future bliss and benefits.

Three times the word Paradise is mentioned in the King James version of the Bible: Luke 23:43; 2 Corinthians 12:4; Revelation 2:7. It is mentioned forty times in the Septuagint version, translated orchard and garden, meaning plenty to see, plenty to eat, to smell, to hear and to enjoy,

the banqueting table filled and sumptuous. It will be the 'fared sumptu-
ously every day' of Luke 16.

The *New Living Bible* gives the words as 'Today you will be with me in
Paradise.' This is a solemn promise. 'This day you will be with Me.' The
Septuagint version of the Old Testament gives it the name of the Garden
of Eden. If this promise fails, all the promises of Jesus fail. If this is correct, and we believe it is, then all the promises are correct.

Jesus rediscovered and redefined Paradise

Richard Chenevix Trench, D.D., writing on the word 'Paradise' says,
'Paradise was a word common in slightly different forms to almost all the
nations of the East, but only as some royal park or garden of delights.' It
became, for the Jew, the first playground of our first parents — the
Garden of Eden. It took Jesus to take the word and sanctify it afresh, to
add new meaning when He used it in Luke 23:43 — the waiting place of
the blissful who have gone on before. Jesus took old, worn out phrases
and added new meaning, reshaping and sharpening them as a sword.
Jesus put flowers and fruits back into Paradise. What might have been a
deserted garden becomes one that is highly significant, sanctified and
made fit for the Master's use by Jesus Christ.

What had long since died in the memories of nations was brought back
from the dead. Jesus used the word, He turned it into what God always
said it should be, a place where God is, where He meets with His creation.
As the Garden of Eden was the resting and raising place of Adam and
Eve before they went into the world, so this Paradise of God is the place
where believers go before entering the new world of Heaven. It is the placing of humanity back among nature, as was God's original intention, to
be the crown of creation, the diamond of His doings and the pearl of His
purposes. That old Garden of Eden in Genesis was a Paradise parade
ground where our first parents were trained for something more, where a
family had its roots. It was there before the curse.

Paradise is a pleasant land

Paradise is a park, a pleasant land, an orchard, a forest of trees[4]. It was
and will be the place of most sublime delight. Remember, it was Jesus

who redecorated, who planted new trees with fresh fruit and all manner of walkways when He made the promise to the thief. The man on the cross said, 'Remember me when You come into your Kingdom.' Jesus made it possible not only to be remembered but to be with Him in Paradise. Jesus will be there, even as God was in the Garden of Eden[5]. Dying is more than becoming a memory. Paradise is part of the Kingdom of Jesus Christ. It is from here that we shall be caught up in a new body, like His glorious body.

Paradise is a Persian pleasure park, where lovers embrace, the altar of town and village. It suggests a walled garden, a very private place equivalent to the Bosom of Abraham. It is the state of grace. There are three places the Jews believed you went to at death, this is one of them[6].

Paradise is a special place

When a Persian king wished to confer a special honour on one who had performed a great deed, allowing such a one into his Paradise was a sort of promotion or recognition that he had been faithful above all. This action of taking into Paradise was rather like the giving of medals for gallantry. The Persian king made him a Companion of the Garden. The champion of the garden made him a companion! The person then had the right to walk through any Royal garden. The secret, the remote, the special and the secluded were his for the joy of entering. All the Palace gardens were his right. If an Army Officer rescued the King's son or won a glorious victory then he was given the right to the fruit trees in the paradise[7]. It was a token of faithfulness. If he caught hold of the general's horse as it pranced and was about to bolt with fear and thus saved the master from injury or certain death, he was given the supreme honour of walking around the gardens with the king. If one made a great discovery that would benefit many, the same introduction was granted. If a mountaineer climbed a great mountain he was honoured in the same way, rather like being invited to Buckingham Palace and being given recognition for some gallant service to humanity. If you were able to solve a problem or a riddle that no-one else was able to solve, the same treatment would be yours. It was, in a measure, what happened to Daniel and Joseph when they interpreted the King's dreams[8]. If an assassination attempt was revealed to the King the reward was to be taken into his secret gardens.

Those people were rewarded for their good works, but our entering into Paradise, as with the thief on the cross, is a matter of grace, not of works. The dying thief had no good works to recommend him. He entered Paradise on and by grace alone. The gate has already been opened by Jesus Christ. After death you will go into this beautiful scented region, surrounded by rare flowers that never wither away, there to behold the goodness and mercy of God, the green pastures of Psalm 23[9]. It will be said to you, with trumpet-like clarity, 'Enter into the joy of your Lord.'

Paradise is the private residence of the King

Originally Paradise was full of meadows, parks and streams, a beautiful landscape garden with all the ornamentation that imagination can grasp. It is a little Psalm 23[9]. It will be as John leaning on the bosom of Jesus. Paradise was the place and the state of the gods. It was part of the summer gardens. It might have been Paradise that Paul mentions when he refers to being caught up into the Third Heaven[10]. The Jews believed there were seven Heavens. The seventh Heaven is the Heaven where we shall dwell forever with our new bodies[11].

Genesis 2:8, 3:1, in the Septuagint version of the Bible, the word Paradise is used of the Garden of Eden. Eden means pleasurable, a delightsome land, a true Beulah of that same name. It is a garden of light, well watered and attended. Mary saw Jesus as the Gardener[12]. Paradise will be without a snake, without temptation. There will be no withering plants, no curse, no cherub with flaming sword, no need to hide behind the tree for shame[13]. We shall be known as we are known. All things will be open before His face. It is a garden beyond compare, even the Mount of Olives has no comparison with this Paradise. The Garden of Gethsemane has no part or lot in this matter. It will be a lakeside leisure centre!

'In my Father's house are many mansions.' Jesus is speaking of the diversity, the multiplicity of the place. Heaven as Paradise will be multiplicity in diversity. There will be no sameness or boredom. Diversity of the tongue is the paradise of that tongue. Language is its love. The multiplication can be Paradise.

Paradise is a secure place

The term Paradise was used by the historian, Xenophon. It is made up of two words meaning 'around' and 'wall'. It is used in the Song of Solomon 4:13. It will be permeated with the scent of flowers and all manner of fruit. There are such dashing colours as armies in varying uniforms. It is called the Paradise of God. Have you been into a real garden lately? Have you visited the place of beauty where it seems mother nature has used step ladders to reach the top of the trees and grandly scaled walls to place ivy in the brightest of green shades? The master botanist, the glorious landscape artist has been at work here! It will not only satisfy you, you will be satisfied, made complete by the awareness of the surroundings. Nothing needs to be added. It will be perfect security and securely perfect. Today in Paradise. What care! What closeness! What company!

Every promise in the Word of God is a bird of Paradise, pointing to future happiness of the highest quality and order. It is where every soldier of the king secretly hoped to be invited, where sword, shield, arrow and spear and uniform are laid aside as dirty linen and where everyone can be themselves.

The meanest will have one thousand servants, and will eat from golden dishes with music such as they have never heard. Every tree is a testimony to God's goodness, every flower a pure arrangement of the glory of God.

When Martin Luther was asked what he would do if he knew that he would die that night he replied, 'I would go into my garden and plant an apple tree.' Paradise is where everything and everybody finds its place, including you.

Paradise is a picture of the pleasure of the Lord

Paradise is the extension of the pleasure of the Lord which was prophesied would prosper in the hand of Jesus Christ[14]. It is the bringing together of all promised blessings, all the literal fruits of the Spirit into one area of life to be enjoyed forever. The boughs will hang lowest where you are. The flower heads and petals will be turned in your direction, releasing scent into the air. The rivers will bend into your place. A farmer sows, the fruit grows, but he longs for the day of the harvest. We shall reap as we faint not. We shall enter into the joy and pleasure of the Lord.

Paradise is part of the laughter of the Lord, an acreage of His wealth.

It is to be where all is best. Fawcett in his *Commentary on the Bible* says, 'Paradise is that which is connected to a mansion.' John 14:3 tells us there is a mansion being prepared for us. Is Paradise the place in which we wait until that mansion is finally complete? It certainly is no back garden, nor part of a tenement or window box. It is more than a herb garden or old allotment, of which we British were so proud in the 1940 War Years!

Paradise is part of Christ's kingdom

The dying thief saw Jesus as King with a Kingdom. Jesus simply gave him part of that Kingdom. This is pressed down, shaken together and running over. The Paradise is different from the thorn bush, the battlefield, the cut and bruise, the wound and the hurt. The fruits and harvest are so different from the plough blade. It is the pleasure after the pain, the crown after the cross. One of the seven ancient wonders of the world was the hanging gardens of Babylon, yet even those are but weeds, weak stemmed flowers when compared with that promised by Jesus Christ. In those Babylonian gardens were flowers of every description.

Whatever our tastes in fruit, then it will be that taste. Whatever scent is best to your nostrils, then that is the scent in the Paradise of God. The main colour will be your colour. Your favourite flower and tree will be there in abundance, still in the ground, still growing, uncut, untouched, reserved for you. They will never fade. Jesus did not mean Paradise to be a mirage but an actual and factual place for you to enter as you slip out of time to walk into Eternity.

Paradise will be filled with the music of delight

A lady had a vision of Heaven, where everything abounded with greenery and blossoming flowers. The remarkable thing was that every flower had a song to sing, everything in the vision was singing. Each stone, each stream had a song.

All the pleasure which the eye can behold, the ear can hear, the mouth can taste is in this Paradise. It is not sensual, but scenic. It will be serenely arranged as part of the Master's mind with you in mind! We still need fruit to taste and trees to climb, valleys and hills with streams to stroll along. Paradise could never be a dead end, a cul-de-sac. It is leading to something larger, something that has been under construction since Jesus arose from the dead. It is not to boredom you are going, but to blessing.

The caricature of the saint on a cloud playing a harp is a mockery from the devil. The future will not be like that. It would be appallingly boring. It is where there is no setting or rising of the sun, trees are ever with fruit, the sun is always at the right heat, everything is clockwork without being mechanical. No pointing fingers, no withering fruit, no night and no need to turn aside from that which God has prepared for those who love Him. To Abraham it was a land of promise. To Israel it was Canaan, to the New Testament believer it is the Paradise of God.

This place of Paradise belongs to God's dedicated ones meaning, in New Testament words, Saints, not in the future, the Saints at Philippi, the Saints at Colosse, the Saints at Rome, but 'the Saints in Paradise'.

We have sought for pleasure in treasure and the things around us but the real pleasures are within, the future found in the Paradise of God. Has anyone returned to tell of this Paradise? No! It is so pleasurable they would not wish to return!

Paradise will exceed every excellence

Take the greatest moment, the sheer delight, the beautiful summer's day and stretch it to last forever. There you have an idea of what Paradise means. Your birth, your birthday, the moment you fell in love for the first time, the best present you ever received, the wearing of that new dress, the moment you were born again and realised your sins were all forgiven — add these together and then add much more. There you may have just an inkling of what Paradise means. Going is the release of the captive, arriving is the end of a long journey, a stepping out of the thought and into the glorious reality, part of resurrection life. It will be the completion of John 10:10, which the *New English Bible* translates, 'I am come that you might have life in all its fullness,' or as in the Book of Joshua 3:15, from the same Bible, 'The Jordan was in full flood.'

If a great discovery is shared, then all benefit. How many will be in Paradise because I have been faithful in my witness?

It will not be Milton's 'Paradise Lost', where he sees himself as a wandering soul. Wanderings will terminate in a known way. You will go through the gate (death) into the garden (Paradise) and into the house (Heaven).

In the Foreword of the old King James Bible there is a reference to the Monarch and all the lands he had conquered which had been added to England. Paradise is part of God's created lands, and part of it has been reserved for you.

The moment you die, or should I say move out of your body, this day you will be in Paradise with Me. Not a soul sleep or a dark night, not a deep and wide grave. There is no mound of earth or waiting time. It is from one thing to the other. Paradise for ever!

NOTES

1. 1 Corinthians 2:9.

2. Hebrews 2:14.

3. Judges 3:20.

4. Dr James Strong, L.L.D., *Gesenius Hebrew-Chaldee Lexicon*, published by Baker Book House, America.

5. Genesis 3:8,10.

6. Chapter Eleven.

7. Revelation 2:7.

8. Daniel 2:48; Genesis 41.

9. See the author's book, *Paths of Righteousness in Psalm 23*.

10. 2 Corinthians 12:2.

11. Chapter Twelve.

12. John 20:15.

13. Genesis 3:10.

14. Isaiah 53:10.

CHAPTER
8

Who Will Take Care of Me in the Future Life?

There is a period of waiting in the future life, a time spent in Paradise, in Abraham's bosom in the immediate presence of God, when we pass from this life into the next. After that time, you will receive a resurrection body which is like the body of Jesus[1], and you will be free for all Eternity to do as Jesus did in that resurrection body. As God prepared a body for Him, so He will do the same for you, that we might be as one with Him[2]. After the resurrection from the dead[3] you will be with the Lord for ever, with a new and glorious body, as a bride attired for her wedding. That time will last forever, longer than space or thought endures, the beginning and the continuation of being with the Lord.

Those who have been 'in' the Lord on earth, will be 'with' the Lord in Heaven for ever. The end of the way after the storm is to be with Christ. It is arriving, being where you have always wanted to be, having what you always wanted to have. It will be such a destination, brought by such a desire, and knowing that all has been accomplished in a life given to Jesus Christ.

Paul makes reference to this for-ever state in 1 Thessalonians 4:17, and in Philippians 1:23. The main emphasis is to be with the Lord. What is said is not simply based on emotion, not as the tide which comes and goes, or an infrequently blowing wind bringing change; it is a complete conviction. Here is the very core of Christianity, the fact that we will be with the Lord for ever. How often have you desired something to last for ever because it is so peaceful, so restful, so useful and eventful? Jesus with us will not be less than He was on earth, but more.

There will be miraculous care

There will be more, much more of the better essentials of Eternal life in Jesus Christ. He will be with one and all together. The Lord fed the five thousand — all needs will be met. Millions will be miraculously cared for. The blind will be healed, the deaf hear, the woman with the spirit of infirmity will be healed. The only bowed things in Heaven will be the rainbow surrounding the Throne and those worshipping or bending to play the harps of gold. The words 'Lo, I am with you always,' will be completely fulfilled. You will be with Me always. He will open His hand and satisfy the desire of every living thing.

There will be nothing in Heaven that is not with Christ. Heaven is large and Jesus fills that largeness, more than fills it, He completes it. He is in every corner and at every turn. Wherever you are, He is there. That is the miracle of Eternity. The sound, the songs, the scenes are all part of Jesus Christ. He is the Eternity you have longed for. The Eternal God is part of that Eternal place which houses an Eternal race.

Those who care and have cared will be cared for

Those things against you will be gone, banished into a billion years of forgetfulness. The atheist and the agnostic and the humanist will go to what they believed in, which is nothing. Theirs will be an empty, shallow eternity, while the believer is filled with the fullness of Jesus Christ. All things are yours, says the Son of God, the God of Heaven.

Heaven is entering into the joy of your Lord. It will be part of the 'pleasures at His right hand for evermore,' in Psalm 16:11. The 'pleasures' are those things that are pleasant and sweet, as pleasant as David's love for Jonathan. Earth's tastes will be sour compared with the nectar of Heaven. It is where the full measures of His river of pleasure flows, in Psalm 36:8; there is delight, for we are in the delightsome land.

It means that there will be no more loneliness, no single sparrow or flower, everything will be married to Him who is the Lord. There will never be the single soul. Widowhood will be no more; the fatherless will have a Father; the orphan a parent, another Comforter. It will be fellowship and presence, seeing with the full eye, hearing with the full ear, fully tasting with the mouth and knowing to full capacity. It will be love at large, a banquet fit for a King. Every step up takes two directions — an impossibility in this life we have now.

The cares of this life will be forgotten in Heaven

There are those who have had visions of Heaven and everything, from sea to leaves and thrones, were all singing. Water was singing water. Every item had a voice with which to sing, such is the music and worship in life after death. Everything in Heaven became a musical instrument or was part of a great choir, which became a trio and then a duet, until out of one mouth came a solo. The voice and the song have been set free. To use Martin Luther King's famous words, 'Free! Free at last!' All the happenings in visions and dreams were musical. Heaven is a place of worship, honour and rejoicing, where God is All in All.

The charisma of Christ will take care of everything

'With' the Lord. John 1:1 says 'In the beginning was the Word, the Word was "with" God.' Meaning alongside, suggesting to be in the bosom, rather like two trees in an orchard or two rivers flowing side by side until their waters merge into one sparklingly pure stream. The various members of your body take care of each other, with the head taking overall care. So Jesus will take care of you as completely as the sun shines on one piece of fruit on the branch of a tree as if it was the only piece in the universe. He will care for you as if you were the only one in Heaven. As an eye in the head you will be in Him.

After struggle there is relaxing, after the birth through death there is Life awaiting. No need to look outside Bible covers for the facts relating to that Life until we are bathed in the very atmosphere of it. It is faith which takes us beyond mental reasonings. The promise of faith will be finalised.

The love of God will remove all cares

The love of God is shaped into harps and musical instruments for your delectation and relaxation. That love appears as palm leaves, angels, thrones, with crowns and pearly gates in the Book of Revelation. Love will be shaped into flowing streams, golden streets and harps. It can never be just singing, it is worshipping. To be there will be glory enough. For the first time you will have space. Others will see the complete workings of grace in your life. The Garden of the Lord will be expanse enough, fulfilling enough.

When the Prodigal Son returned, the Father had bread enough and to spare. Heaven will be enough and to spare. When Jacob returned to meet Esau his brother, he said, 'I have enough[3]'. The word means 'all'. It will never be said, 'What are these among so many?[4] With your name in the Lamb's Book of Life[5] there is a place marked out in the vast Eternity of God. As Man Friday, in the book *Robinson Crusoe*, left a footprint on the sands, so you will make your mark in Heaven.

There will be no need to care about your place in Heaven

The believer will not be cast as some wandering star careering into blackness forever, wobbling along like some loose wagon wheel. Those who belong to Christ on earth will belong to Him in Heaven. To be with Christ is the answer to every question. It is light to darkness, a light which can never go out. Trust Him now and see what He provides then! Love Him here and receive love from Him here and in the hereafter. Write 'Emmanuel' — God with us — over all your life. Then were the disciples glad when they saw the Lord[6].

The living and loving Christ becomes the caring Christ

More than the fact that He lived in Bethlehem is the fact that He will live in Heaven! 'Because I live, you will live also'.[7]

When the disciples were with Christ on earth they were benefactors of every miracle. They tasted the sweet wine of Cana, partook of the bread and fish that fed the five thousand; smelled the aroma of the broken box of alabaster ointment; tasted the water at the well of Samaria. The women who ministered to Jesus of their substance ministered to every disciple. They shared the Upper Room. Christ's moments in the Mount were their moments also. What was blessed by Him was enjoyed by them.

If you have entered into the sufferings of Christ on the Cross through salvation, so will you partake of the blessings of Eternity, pressed down, shaken together and running over! Heaven is God's place, His Palace, for His people.

God's creative ability removes all care

God will share His creative ability and heart. Just as He shared it in the feeding of the five thousand so He will share it with you[8].

A life that has been lived in sin will go as coal to the fire, straw to the flame, and shrivel into a naked existence. Jesus loved Mary, Martha and Lazarus and that love will spread throughout Eternity. The advert 'large enough to cope, small enough to care,' says it all. The closeness of Christ will not bring the cry of 'Depart from me, for I am a man of unclean lips.' Every part of Heaven is evidence of His unfailing love. His tenderness is seen in all that is awaiting. As a Church we are the Bride of Christ. The promise to Abraham was that his seed would be as the sand on the seashore, and as the stars of Heaven.[9]

To be in Heaven is to be as carefree as the stars

Each star has a glory all its own. This suggests an earthly people, the Jews, but also a Heavenly people, of which you are one. You are a miracle, a creation, more than a thought. Healing, caring, ministering are all part of the tenderness of Jesus Christ. It will be as the lamb brought in from winter, bottle fed by the fire in the home. All the heart and attention of the shepherd is given to it. You will be so close to Christ — 'They shall see His face'[10]. Show us the Father and we shall be satisfied[11]. Another translation is 'Show us the Father and that will be enough.' We shall be complete.

There would be concern if Jesus was not in Heaven

Note, it would not be Heaven if Jesus was not there. To awake and see the sights of Heaven — the sea of Heaven turned into glass; to breathe the air of Heaven, to find conversation as you lean on the Everlasting Arms! What must it be like to step on a shore and to find it is Heaven's shore? To take hold of a hand and to discover it to be the hand of God! To breathe celestial air, to find immortality, to rise from the care, loneliness and turmoil of earth into unbroken calm; to wake and find glory?[12]

That which surrounds you is Heaven. Without Jesus the circle would be broken, Heaven would be the blackness of outer darkness, a real hell. Hell is a place without Christ.

Heaven will be a time of resting and knowing

John rested on the Bosom of Jesus at the Last Supper and that closeness will be continued. It will be the relationship of the vine and the branch, the shepherd and sheep, builder and stone, the gardener and the rose. It will be the same closeness of John 6, where Jesus said, 'I and the Father are one.' He prayed, in John 17, 'That where I am there they might be also.' The sheep of the other fold will have been brought into one fold. Heaven is the fold of God, and all are safely gathered in. No need then for another face, another smile or another word. Jesus is the full expression of God[13], and He will be the interpretation of that expression in Heaven.

There will only be one language in Heaven, the language of life and of love. All will be heard, all told, all revealed. Truth speaking, truth commending, truth holding court. In the earthly existence there have been many opportunities to get closer to God. Some wish it was not true, for others it will be communication from the Great White Throne. For those who love God it will be heartfelt communication. Every puzzle will find its missing piece. Every mist will lift and the shoreline will be seen. There will be a parting of the clouds and the mystery will become that which is marvellous.

When they said to Alexander the Great: 'The man who can untie that rope, which has been tied with a secure and secret knot, will be a ruler,' Alexander simply took his sword and slashed the rope in half.

There will be no Parables or problems in Heaven. It will be one great joyous Psalm, because His palm was nailed to a Roman frame. The biggest problem at the moment for those living on earth is getting there!

You will be cared for as the shepherd cares for sheep

There will be a leader of the flock in Eternity. There will be no hills to climb without a leader, a source of inspiration. Never to be without a shepherd or out on a dark night without a light, never to be found drifting. Here, we get lost and cannot find our way. In the brightness of this day all will be known. Knowledge and tongue, song and saying will be perfect.

The ugliness of earth will disappear in the beauty of Heaven. The hurt and the pain will be so far removed it may never have been. The dimness and the dark corners of earth will be lost in the pure radiancy of light. It is a scientific fact that if you could travel with a wave of light there would be no time. Where the Light of the World is, there will be no time. It will be a continuation of Christ in every corner.

It will be for evermore

The guide will not leave you to carry your own baggage, there will be no hireling to look after you. God shall be their God. His communication will be as when He spoke with Moses face to face. 'I will be their God.' The Cross of Christ marks everything out on the map. Heaven will be a known place. Those with perfect knowledge will be there, and you will be part of the Infinite. What He says will be timeless truth. His face will outshine all.

His face is as the signature of the artist on the painting, the author on his writings, a witness to His creative ability. There is one face you will instantly recognise, it will be a little like the face of your mother, or your partner, the face of your nearest and dearest, the one you trust the most. All will be in that face, the face of love, joy and peace. The lowliness and loveliness of grace will be that face.

When Satan is unmasked the ungodly will proclaim, 'Is this he who deceived the nations?'

When we see the King in His beauty we shall proclaim, 'This is the Architect of it all, the Designer and the Builder. Here is the wisdom and justice of God.'

The very nature of God is to care for you

The very nature of God will speak in a thousand tongues, yet all will understand and appreciate what He has done. The proverb still applies, 'Round pegs will not fit into square holes.' God will not allow thorns on apple trees. There are biblical lists of those who will not enter Heaven.[14]

Pilgrim, in *Pilgrim's Progress*, said, 'Set my name down there.' There will be no second chance after death. As a tree falls, there shall it be. That which was contrary to God's nature will not be in Heaven. A wreck in the midst of perfection is unacceptable! That which is entering Heaven has been planned, measured, sometimes chopped and sawn, turned and shaped so that it might find its place in the mansions beyond. Each precious jewel speaks of tremendous suffering of the inhabitants, they are the jasper, carbuncle and pearl in Revelation Chapters 21 and 22. All the materials will have passed through the hand of the Carpenter of Nazareth.

Never again to be worn out with the weariness of care

Every tree knows its own fruit, every seed follows a principle after its own kind. The same applies to Heaven. We will not be there because of merit but because of the majesty of His might and grace. Every hollow will be filled, all the waste places will blossom as the rose.

One man was explaining to an Arab how, with modern technology, the whole of the desert could be cultivated. The Arab, looking glum replied, 'But we need the desert!' There are some who will be forever satisfied with things as they are! They are living and dying, instead of Dying and Living!

There will be no mountains or valleys. God will have created everything to fit into the perfect picture, including us when we repent and believe and receive the righteousness of Jesus Christ through faith. There are no Churches, no denominations, in Heaven. It will be the marks of the cross not the doctrines of a denomination! Redemption will be everywhere. They will not sleep as we sleep. They will not grow old as we grow old, but will be forever as the dawning light, the shining sun, rising to set no more.

The wood, straw, hay, stubble of 1 Corinthians 3 will not be there. The slate or rock, pebble or brick find no place or consolation. God's creation finds it setting within that new creation. Those things of a higher quality will come together, made such by the Gospel. Jesus Christ will be accounted as gold, silver, precious stones, crystal clear waters. Each stone has a message, has gone through a process, until it is usable in this United Kingdom of all time and Eternity. Pain becomes pearl. Armouries become Amens.

There will be no care about the future

To be ever with the Lord means that we shall live on. Nothing will ever change that relationship of oneness and closeness. Nothing dies when it is part of God.

The prayer of Jesus in John 17 will be fulfilled. 'Father, I will that they also, whom You gave Me, be with Me where I am, that they may behold My glory!' The glory of how it is all accomplished. The glory of the worship. The glory of the immensity, the glory of utter perfection.

The Heaven above can commence on the earth below as we are born again of God's Spirit.[15] We receive the earnest of Heaven[16], the engagement ring of what is to be, the pledge. There is a call out from sin and a call into the light of life. An upward call, a longing such as migratory birds have when the time is right. They go to warmer climes where they will better fit in. Everything in Eternity will be deepened and sweetened by the presence of Jesus Christ. In Heaven is a new creation. We receive the earnest when we believe.[16] It will be abundant life, expressed in all its fullness.

No-one is lost when they are cared for by Christ

No-one who dies in Jesus is lost. Faith overcomes fate. It holds intact. We know where they are because we know Who He is. We are persuaded that He is able to keep that which is committed unto Him against that day. When we die, it might seem as if we are cast over the side into the watery brink, but it will be the putting out of the net over the right side, at the command of Jesus. It will be the launching out into the deep of His care. John 21:4, 'When morning has come, Jesus stood on the shore.' You can write that on any grave stone!

Death is not the extinguishing of the lamp. The light is put out because the dawn and the day have arrived. The artificial is no longer required. Philippians 1:21 (*Twentieth Century New Testament*) states, 'And in this confidence we would gladly leave our body and make our home with the Lord.' Heaven is the perfect day, the day to end all days, all based on the Ancient of Days Himself.

Oliver Cromwell wrote a book, the last chapter of which was entitled 'Death'. It contained three words: TO BE CONTINUED. As he lay dying he asked, 'Is there no-one who will praise the Lord?'

The books in the New Testament never come to an end, they are continued in living epistles, written by the Holy Spirit — the lives of those who love the Lord. If all the books in the world could not contain the miracles and the mind of Jesus Christ, how many books would it take to convey all the facts about Heaven? Heaven will be a continuation of Acts 1:1, 'Of all that Jesus began to do and teach.' It is the continuation of the former treatise.

The American Indians expressed duration and permanence when they signed treaties with the words 'As long as the river flows, the grass grows and the mountains stand.' Heaven will be longer than that! It will endure forever.

Luke 23:46 is quoted from Psalm 31:5: 'Into Thy hands I commit My spirit.' Every Jewish mother taught her boy to say that prayer at night time. It was the first prayer he learned.

The abundance of Heaven will blot out all care

Let us look at the fullness of metaphors that are used to describe this Heaven, realising that a metaphor is an exchange of one thing for another. A lesser figure can be used for a greater. Metaphors are windows through which we gaze and admire. Sometimes the meaning is heightened, as we say, for example, 'as sweet as sugar or sour as vinegar'.

It is Paradise restored, 2 Corinthians 12:2,4. It is a city, Hebrews 11:16; 13:14, whose walls are salvation and whose gates are praise. A country (fatherland), Hebrews 11:16. A temple, Revelation 3:12; 7:15. A garner, Matthew 3:12. A Kingdom, Ephesians 5:5; 2 Peter 1:11. An inheritance, 1 Peter 1:4. A rest, Hebrews 4:9. God's dwelling place, God's Throne, Father's house. It is a harbour, it is resting in a Bosom[17], city, a temple, a building. It is where Jesus Christ is Sovereign Lord. It is to be with Christ which is better. Jesus is the key to the city gates. You will enter freely or you will not enter at all.

John Newton, author of 'Amazing Grace' said, 'There will be three wonders in Heaven to me...to meet someone I had not expected to see there; to meet someone I had expected to see; and the third, the greatest wonder of all, will be to find myself there!'

All come through repentance, through the receiving of the finished work of Christ on the cross. They are part of 'I make all things new.' A donkey for a burden, a bird for flight, a tree for fruit, and you as a Christian for Heaven. You were born again for this. You were brought into the Kingdom for such a time as this. Grace to adorn, flowers to beautify, but Heaven for the believer to grace.

F. W. Boreham[18] in one of his many books tells the story of the young cricketer who had a blind father. The day the father died the son was playing in a famous match and everyone wondered if the death of his father would affect his playing. He played the game of his life and, when questioned, he replied, 'For the first time ever today my father saw me play cricket!' It is not whether we win or lose, it is how we played the game.

One native group always had their tombs facing west, for death meant the setting of the sun for them. When Christ and His resurrection was preached to them those tombs were turned to face East, where the sun arose!

One of the Christian martyrs was tied to the stake and, as they proceeded to light the wood beneath and around him, he looked to the skies and said, 'You take from me what I cannot keep, and bestow a life upon me that I cannot lose.'

Dying is Living!

P.S. Will I see YOU in Heaven?

NOTES

1. Philippians 3:21; 1 John 3:1–3.

2. Hebrews 2:10; 10:5.

3. Genesis 33:11.

4. John 6:9,10.

5. Revelation 21:27.

6. John 20:20.

7. John 11:25,26.
8. John 6:9–13.
9. Genesis 22:17; 32:12.
10. Revelation 22:4.
11. John 14:8.
12. Author unknown.
13. Hebrews 1:1–3.
14. 1 Corinthians 6:9; Ephesians 5:5; 1 Timothy 1:10; Revelation 21:8.
15. John 3:7.
16. 2 Corinthians 1:22; 5:5.
17. See Chapter Eleven.
18. Methodist Minister and writer from the last century.

CHAPTER
9

How Will Death Affect Me?

When Elijah was transported to Heaven it was the ending of a great life on earth and the beginning of a new life in Heaven. God never made anything which led nowhere. It is from here to Eternity! The whole span of a life, the miracles, the wondrous deeds, challenging kings and establishing the Kingdom of God in Israel was reduced to two verses, found in 2 Kings 2:11,12. What God had put so much into He sent for and took to Heaven.

The manner of your death does not matter, nor does the timing of it, the important thing is to know that the great Lord who cared for you on earth will carry you to Heaven. From earth to Heaven is about the span of the hand of God. Heaven is nearer than you think. The finest miracle in the life of Elijah was at death, it was a miracle for the prophet of miracles.

Death does not affect God's care for us

We can spend a life caring for and loving others and, at death, God cares for His own as His own throne. There was no taking Elijah into Eternity as a lamb, for he had been more like a lion in his nature and understanding. The power which has been with you all your life will continue. Like the old films I used to watch which ended 'to be continued'. It is God who draws the sheet over a life. The bus came to where the Stop was. It was in the form of a chariot of fire, and it knew where to go. Elijah was taken in a loving, moving horse-galloping chariot. It was the going out of the Light Brigade.

It might be an angel for you, or the soft shoulder of a shepherd if you are a lamb. There is no limiting God's caring nature to this life or to the after life. Big in this life, even bigger in the after life. Grace comes from God. Love, kindness, help and mercy, all are from God. That which took the shape of an Ark with Noah, became as a rod in the hand with Moses, even becoming inspiration in the Psalms, now takes the shape of a chariot with horses. The wind had been part of his life and through a whirlwind he was taken up into Heaven. Where he might have been walking or even limping with old age he found himself travelling in style. The One Who parts the waters, parts life from death.

How we live does affect how we are redeemed

These two verses (2 Kings 2:11,12) are the epitaph that God wrote on Elijah's life, a living epitaph. His death, his disappearing was as dramatic as his living. The man who had lived so dramatically died in the same manner. God sent the emblems of his life, fire, horse and chariot and wind in a whirlwind. It took a larger miracle to take him home than he ever saw in his life. God wrote what He thought of him in miracle form, as the chariot raced in to take him out, rather like our modern helicopter! What we are clothes us at death. We arrive there as we were in life. Scripture becomes the eye of the Almighty through which we see life.

Passing over the waters may be less dramatic for you, but God will arrange that which conveys you into His presence, to live on after the power of an endless life. There were no stops for this chariot. It went on and on.

Death does affect those around you

It is good that, apart from all other mourners, there are Heavenly guests and moving objects present at death. Elijah, along with Enoch, attended his own funeral! God did all the arranging. It was swift, it was sure, it was dynamic, it was ongoing. He was almost snatched out of this world. God came to take what was His very own. We are His very own people.[1] You rejoice at a birth but mourn at a death because you are not the one in the coffin. The two extremes of life are napkin and coffin.

Elijah was different in that his death and his funeral took place at the same time. Again, it was different in that he never died. He was but a symbol, simply a shadow, a little sketch of the death and living on of every believer. The horses didn't trample him underfoot; the chariot wheels didn't run over him; the fire didn't burn him or the wind blow him apart. What the prophet needed to get to Heaven was God-sent and God-given, there was an upward lift in love. He was taken as part of the nation's heart. So live and die that you leave friends looking for you. So loved, that flowers are tear shaped.

As Elijah approached death he passed through so many things which held sacred memories for him. It is good to have fond memories of spiritual happenings. Those things which are essential to life here were taken, as those around him felt the pain of parting. So live that no-one can fill your shoes!

There is part of us which death does not affect

Elijah was still walking, talking, working and fellowshipping. Whilst you are on earth there is an empty chariot. Here death is seen as going into a chariot. The man of God stepped into it, he didn't fall into it or faint into it. He blessed another believer in his death, he left something worth having in a 'double anointing' that was passed on in a cloak. He entered into what would be our modern Rolls Royce — Heaven's chariot for earth's treasure.

A coffin was being transported in a Rolls Royce and a young man was heard to say, 'Boy, that's the way to be buried.' Unfortunately the body was dead and the car engine quite still. There was no life after death in the scene, no spirited horses, no emblems of life, just an open grave. Elijah the prophet, fully clothed, seated and in his right mind disappeared, to reappear and remain.

Death does not affect truth

When we are buried that is not everything. We may bury the rags, we may bury your remains, but the you, the character within you has long since been taken away and laid where they know not. There is that in your life which is deeper than the grave and higher than the Heavens. Elijah did not know the flickering eyes, the shallow breathing, the fight, the shortage of breath. It was like a fish in a stream — from the goldfish bowl to the mighty ocean. There was a vast expanse before him and God provided the bridge, but he didn't have to walk one step of the way. Each step was in the pulling of the horse, the moving of the chariot. Something was produced, as it will be produced for you, which Elijah didn't have to provide.

It isn't always angels that are sent to carry us.[2] God as the King of Heaven sent out His personal chariot for Elijah. His death became the birth, the nativity of future hopes. If one man can pass through death, we can all pass through it. His chariot and his life needed a new direction. It required to travel further than earth.

Death does not affect God's best for us[3]

God kept God kept His best until the last. To die a believer is to have chariot and horses. It is to have provision in this life and in the life to come. His Lord had that in waiting, prepared and ready. Not the sluggish, the broken, the corrupt, but the best. The chariot was chosen without wobbly wheel or weak axle.

After the Mount Carmel experience Elijah went to a higher mountain — Eternity. After drought conditions he went where the fountain of water is sweet. From being threatened by Jezebel[4], feeling faint, even having a nervous breakdown[5], he went into the Pacific (peace) of God. The chariot wheels turned and the horses galloped. Elijah went as one going into battle. You are not finished at death, neither has God finished with you. There is still more. When you switch the engine off, the car has still much more mileage.

Death does not affect future visions and completion

There are new things ahead. Elijah never rode in the King's chariot, so God granted him one instead! This mode of transport was a combination of two horses and a chariot. Elijah did not have to get out the do-it-yourself kit! You will not have to do anything, it is all done, has been done by Jesus Christ.[6] Elijah wasn't left with a battered old coat and a swelling Jordan river. These horses were vigorous with life. Horses and chariots are a perfect combination. It wasn't a vehicle that no one else wanted, it didn't come from the scrapyard. God sends His best. He sent Jesus, and He will send angels to attend our death as He sent them for Lazarus[7]. No-one seemed to know where he was[8], but Elijah knew, God knew, and you will know. While you are present down here you are absent up there.

We do not all die but are carried by angels into Abraham's bosom. God has many ways of conveying us to Heaven. As each fruit tree bears its own manner of fruit, so God has His own way of taking us, some swiftly, some softly, but you will be taken, not simply into an extension of what you have now, but into a new form of life. This will not be a continuation of existence but an unfolding of a dream, probably the only dream you ever had which will come true, as true as when Joseph dreamed he saw those bowing down before him[9].

Death does not affect the power of God

There can be dramatic acts at death. Elijah was living loose, without experiencing loose living. Only a coat and a river before him. God took him across the river. 2 Kings 2:8 is typical of all who die. They have to pass through the waters of death. The life of Jesus has prevailed in severing those waters.

When Christian in *Pilgrim's Progress*[10] came to the River of Death he found what he thought was deep was in fact shallow, and angels came out of the City to convey him over.

Elijah didn't die in the river, he went beyond it, for the river was parted[11]. He was taken away, not thrown away. It wasn't a watery grave in the river but a crossing to the other side. There is no dark wet river waiting for you. Most rivers, the people of God had to cross in the Bible were parted by the power of God, and the people went through on dry land[12]. Both the living and the dying pass through the waters by the same means, the righteousness of Jesus Christ, His life on earth and death on a cross. He is the bridge over troubled waters. Death to some may be as the bridge in Venice, The Bridge of Sighs, which leads from prison to the gallows. Through Jesus Christ it is the Bridge of Sights and Sounds. We pass through a dull world into a world of bright music, for the singing of the birds has come.

Death does not affect zeal

Elijah proved, right at the end, that his heart had grown neither cold nor old. There was nothing stagnant about him. He was carried into Heaven, going on with God. Many have passed into the future singing. One dying saint was heard to whisper 'Bring! Bring!' They mentioned a number of things she might be asking for. She finally completed the sentence by saying 'Bring forth the Royal diadem and crown Him Lord of all!'

The fragrance of his first love was dispersed around. God was in that chariot, the man of God did not have to drive into Heaven. You don't drive what is sent for you. I don't think the horses were black, more of a pink colour. There is nothing black about going to Heaven! There was a red flame of sparkle and beauty, colourful, wonderful. The colours of Heaven are variegated. If not, then when you see me in Heaven, tell me!

There was fellowship of a fuller nature ahead. Previously it had been between Elijah and Elisha and it might have become a little pedantic, predictable and boring. Elijah was replaced by God. It could be written after this event — they two went on[13] meaning God and Elijah. All the learning of earth was placed in that chariot. It was quite different to a coffin. It was more a frame for a picture, a chest for treasure. It had its own wheels. What a contrast between some of our undertakers and these fiery horses! This is surely a better way to go. The writer to the Hebrews says, God has provided for us something better[14].

Death does not affect God's provision

If the transport be a chariot, angels, the hand of God or the arm of Jesus, even those clothed in white as cherubim or some other form which takes us at death into the presence of the Lord, then it does not matter. Chariots racing might frighten you. God will send just what suits you and will neither harm nor alarm. There was a fullness of fact, not less, but more. Remember, the chariot was the swiftest moving vehicle they knew in their day. God sent the best for the best of earth. It was a Royal hand which picked this fruit from a Royal tree in the Royal garden, for the life of Elijah was so different to those around him. He believed God and God always surrounds faith with facts. The best transport came to catch him away, to take him up.

It wasn't just an horse or a chariot of fire which took him to Heaven, there was also a whirlwind. In Job 38:1, God sends answers and speaks to us out of one. In Jeremiah 4:13, God is seen operating in a whirlwind as if it is part of His nature, power and authority. In Habakkuk 3:14, God has His way in a whirlwind. Not a zephyr, not a gentle sea breeze, not a quiet wind, but a whirlwind. The very term whirlwind means to rush upon with great force. When we cannot go any further, God blows us along in a wind. Like seed in the wind Elijah was carried away.

Death need not affect our fellowship

Conversations were as deep as the water they passed through. They two went on. Elisha did not cut himself off from the familiar friend. When you really believe you want to surround yourself with other believers. Elijah wanted his successor to be there at the end. Those things which have been familiar stay with us. He was going to a fellowship of more than two — an innumerable company, the hosts of Heaven. At the other side of the river the chariot swung low. Heaven is a deeper, wider, more embracing fellowship that awaits. One becomes many, and many become a multitude, until John in the Book of Revelation sees a number which no man could number[15].

This is the giving of yourself to another. He laid himself, placed himself in that which was sent by God. If God is driving, then you need to be trusting. By faith we step in and go through death into the higher realm. He went higher and further in death than he ever went in life. This scene was full of activity with not one tear or flower in sight. There were no mourners, only praisers. The real last will and testament of this prophet was in Elisha who had received his teachings. He still talked, still had something to give (2 Kings 2:11).

Death does not affect our faith

Elijah believed in the end and he believed for the end, that it might be a beginning. There was no darkness, horses of fire illuminated the way like burning brands with legs. What finishes on earth for you can be the start in another realm. The last furrow had been ploughed, but wait and see, there is yet to be a harvest! He knew God would come for him. He went out believing, he went up believing, he went on believing God. He went through with his faith intact. His faith connected his life to God's chariot. His faith reached out and placed him in God's chariot.

Trust trusts God's transport. It has a free ride into the Eternity of God which is more than a fistful of gold. Faith recognised what God had organised. Faith lit the fire and turned the chariot wheels to face towards

Heaven and God. The presence of God was the stable to the horses. The Egyptians used to paint famous victories on the sides of the chariots. I wonder what was painted on the side of Elijah's? By appointment to the King! I wonder what will be painted on yours? Think of all your, perhaps quiet, but famous, victories! In God the fly overcomes the spider!

Horses breathing fire didn't shatter or lessen, didn't burn him or make him let his faith go. The wind, horse, chariot and fire were the essentials of his faith, still moving, still glowing, still in rein. When you let the reins go loose then the strong hands of God will take those same reins. We go to Heaven in and on God's chariot.

Note, there was no fear. There was no trembling when the chariot of fire and the horses came. They were driven by God in a whirlwind. God, through faith, brought more to the man of God of what he was. He went from feet walking and river crossing to chariot riding. Death is seen as a free ride in a chariot.

Death does not affect the memory of familiar things

There are certain views and scented moments we carry with us. Elijah went from one thing to another accepting death as if he was letting his own son into his house. He took with him to Heaven all his memories of earth, there to be shared like gold among kings. He had been associated with Ahab's chariot. How he must have longed for a ride in it sometimes. With weary feet after much travel, God gives him a ride. God will lift you up and take you in. Earth's views and memories dimmed when Heaven's full capacity was revealed. Memory is God's deposit box. It is the ear for the earring. Let me have my memories, but unfaded, unclouded, let me see them in Heaven's light.

In life we run with the chariot, we walk with it, in death we ride in it. It might have been something Elijah had always wanted to do, and that which is denied on earth is introduced into Heaven. During his lifetime there would be no room in kings' chariots for Elijah. They were kept for the great, not for the small. All God's people have a chariot, provided by God which will take them out of this world. It was the best piece of equipment for the purpose. Heaven will be what suits you the best, made to measure. God makes chariots fly! The constraints of earth were removed, the downward pull was no longer there. As we go towards Heaven that which faith has built does not crumble. Had the prophet ever been in the King's royal chariot? Moving over the rough terrain he might have fallen over or fallen out. God's vehicle does not shake or sway from side to side because of the uneven surface, for it does not touch the earth, other than for a moment to catch away the man. This is part of God's space programme!

Death does not stop us going forward

Elijah stepped into another dimension. Instead of worn out shoes and aching feet he has a chariot. He had gone on and through the water but now he must ascend on high. Whatever the conversation, the end had to be completed above. It was a chariot with fresh horses and there is no end to the pathway of God. The Milky Way opened up. This was only one of God's vehicles. We see through a glass darkly[16]. Like Alice in Wonderland you cannot spend your life going through a looking glass. There has to be something of reality. We cannot go through life with both feet in the air. Death has to be faced but if I can face it with a chariot which can out-run, and out-manoeuvre it, then there is no fear. Doubts and fears are left behind as we speed onward. There is a way through for you.

Elijah was not left where he disappeared. It wasn't an end, it wasn't horses and chariot going down a steep cliff or off the end of the pier. They were stabled in the power of God and like faithful horses they were bound for their stable. It was a journey with fresh beasts pulling. Psalm 23 says 'Goodness and mercy shall follow me all the days of my life'.[17] C. H. Spurgeon depicted these two as the footmen on the stage coach. Their work was to see to each stage of the journey and to provide fresh horses. God's goodness and mercy will do that for you. Thank God Elijah crossed the river not down like a stone but up like a bird, ascending in the ascendancy of the Son.

2 Kings 2, verse 11: They didn't stop short. All that Heaven is he entered into, where celestial bodies revolve, the higher realm. There was more mileage before him than he had ever travelled. He didn't walk, limp run or jump, he was driven to Heaven. Heaven will be such a contrast to our walking, stumbling, hurting down here.

It was Peter in Acts 10 who saw the white sheet lowered and lifted again. It was the place of release, when the golden bowl is broken and the silver thread is snapped.[18] Not so with Elijah. He went to the place of release.

Death does not affect our love

It did not put the fire out. It shaped it into what he needed the most to lift him into the presence of God, surrounding him as horses and a chariot. The blowing whirlwind kept him going. Life and passing through the waters had not blown his fire out. This was his second wind. He went out burning, even as he had lived. This was not now God answering by fire on an altar but by Him meeting the need of the moment. This same God will come to collect you. God will take His jewels and put them in a safe place where thieves cannot break through and steal, moth and rust cannot corrupt.

Elijah's love on earth had been for God. Every action, every moment of challenge or of boldness had sprung out of his love for God. It had been as a reserve, ready for action, ready to be activated. Now this love is depicted in a whirlwind, a moving, racing chariot and turning wheels. There is a strength about it. Death will not put out your love for God but it will add to it, seeing all you have been believing. Blind eyes will be opened, will blink at the brightness of the celestial light. It will be knowing all that you have been trusting for. May your love arrive in the Heavenly realm not as something worn out or cast off, but as these horses, fire, wind and chariot. Even as the Prodigal Son when he returned home received his first coat, may you be fully clothed upon. Love can be as ardent as a prancing, pawing horse, ready to race, ready to chase and challenge the wind.

It was a chariot of fire which came, it was alive and burning and would show the way through any darkness.

Death does not affect or rob us of a future

There was more on the other side of the river than on this side. There was more up above than there was down below. We forget, sometimes, that life is made up not simply of left and right but above and below. Some spend all their lives looking right and left. There must be marvellous goals even in Heaven. There was more for Elijah to reach for in God. What happened for this man of God can and will happen for you. There is more ahead. There are more blessings, more excitements, more endeavours, until your cup is full and running over. There is more beyond, much more in the higher regions. The journey of life did not end in death. Death was a springboard into something more. When going on a journey you take some form of transport. What car can take you into the future? God can, and will. Wait a while — the future you believed for will be more than you expected. You take your coat off when starting a job. You enter into a chariot when you are going somewhere.

Elijah illustrates what will happen at the resurrection in 1 Thessalonians 4:17, 1 Corinthians 15. He also illustrates what happens when we depart this life, or, as the Salvation Army would say, are 'Promoted to Glory'.

The Targum says, 'His prayers were better to Israel than horses or chariots.' His life was one great battlement. His life was armour, spear, shield, horse and chariot. He left his emblem in a living thing. It wasn't written in stone or arranged in flowers, it lives on in all who are spiritual. Elijah sat in the front of his own hearse! He was as much in control in death as ever he was in life. When the chariot is love, the horses peace, provision, kindness and gentleness, with grace and hope then all is well. These beasts were not dromedaries running from side to side, they were horses running in a straight line. The chariot wasn't empty. Death was filled with fire, with the Presence of God. Wheels were turning, it was all happening. This wasn't the chariot with broken wheels as the chariots of Pharaoh[19]. God will plan that for you in such a measure. The chariot may be different, but God will be the same.

It was a ride, a march of triumph. Elijah was as one on a lap of honour. A victory drive! He has left us with much inspiration.

Living or dying does not affect the fact that we belong to the Lord

It was God who came, wrapped in a whirlwind. What a way to go! Elijah's last pulpit was one of fire. God sent fire, the emblem of holiness, to take him to Heaven.

God will send that which suits us. A shovel or a spade are but poor substitutes. Spades and sceptres are both buried in graves. If you have been zealous for God, then a chariot and horse inside a ball of fire with a wind blowing will not matter. A snail to the snail, a gentle dove to the gentle dove. As in life, so in death God understands the nature of the transport we need. For the New Testament believer at the resurrection it will be a trumpet, the voice of the archangel.[20]

In Preston, Lancashire, in 1994 there was a competition to see who had the loudest voice. It will be Jesus Christ, 1 Thessalonians 4:17: 'The Lord Himself shall descend.' All His miracles await us in Heaven. The strength, purpose and wisdom of His being will all be at our disposal. You go as you are, and arrive as you will, because you belong to the Lord. That which binds is drawn tenderly. He comes to carry you away, wounded out of the battle.

The hymn 'That will be glory for me' was composed to remind the writer of his friend, Ed Card. He was always shouting 'Glory'. He was known as 'Glory face'.

H. G. Wells writing in his *First Men on the Moon*, said, 'You cannot fit Heaven into earth. The phenomena of Heaven cannot be fitted into the language of the earth. They can only be a caricature of the real.'

A Christian lady was dying and her minister said to her, 'I am sorry.' 'Don't be sorry,' she replied, 'I am going over the river and my Father owns the land on both sides.'

Death does not affect what we have been and what we have done

Death does not paint everything in the black of despair. Hope Eternal springs up into everlasting life. Your accomplishments remain not as crumbs but as whole loaves, multiplied by the Master's hands. Death for the Christian is the Honourable Discharge from the battle. Elijah went out of life quicker than he came into it. Matthew Henry wrote: 'He who has his head in Heaven need not fear to put his feet into the grave.'

Death is not something that just happens to you. It is that which God makes for you. It is as much part of His timepiece as the dawn or a star. J. A. Motyer penned these wonderful words, 'Death is not the end. It is not even the beginning of the ending, it is the beginning of the beginning.'

The strong belief that we shall never die is the light for the darkness and the chariot for weary feet. Elijah did not walk, he rode, he went in style. When we spend our lives walking in the Way we are called to ride into Heaven. The Roman Appian Way becomes the Milky Way — the pathway to the gods! Elijah lived as a peasant and soared as an angel. He went into the royal palace, in a royal vehicle provided by the Royal King.

NOTES

1. John 10:14; 17:10.
2. Luke 16:22; 24:4.
3. Philippians 1:21–23.
4. 1 Kings 19:2.
5. 1 Kings 19:1–4.
6. John 19:30; John 14:1–3.
7. Luke 16:22.
8. 2 Kings 2:16,17.
9. Genesis 37:5–8.
10. *Pilgrim's Progress*, by John Bunyan.
11. 2 Kings 2:14.
12. Exodus 14; Joshua 3:15–17.
13. 2 Kings 2:2,4,6.
14. Hebrews 7:7,19,22; 9:23; 10:34.
15. Revelation 5:11; 7:9.
16. 1 Corinthians 13:12.
17. See author's book, *Paths of Righteousness in Psalm 23*.
18. Ecclesiastes 12:6.
19. Exodus 14:25.
20. 1 Thessalonians 4:17.
21. *Quotable Quotes*, by Anthony B. Castle.

CHAPTER
10

Will God Be With Me in the Future?

We have looked at those who died and were buried, but now we must turn our attention to those who had no epitaphs or graves. If you examine their lives closely you will find that they were happy, holy, and Heavenly. If you look at their lives with the blind eye of unbelief, you will see nothing. If you listen with ears dull of hearing there is no call from them to you, no hearing of the angelic choir after death.

There are some who gaze into the Old Testament looking for life after death as a man gazing into a muddy pool waiting to catch sight of his own reflection. There are those who illustrate life after death as revealed in the New Testament, there as pillars, not of salt, but of hope; as archways and gates of pearl into God's Eternal City; there as the 'pointer stars' pointing forward, onward and upward into the presence of God. It is from such people that we seek a city whose builder and maker is God. He is the architect and the arranger of it all. There is so much more about Heaven in Heaven's Book.

In Bury, Lancashire there is a seat overlooking the town called 'The Pleasant View'. There are breathtaking vistas in God's Word.

God is larger than life

The God who is large enough to take of this life with all its manifested forms, from seed to sapling, egg to entity, is also capable enough of taking care of all future forms of life. He is big enough to cope, yet small enough to care. God never intended to limit, crush or rub out personalities at death. His intention is to release into something of everlasting value. Even the sparrow may be caught and placed in a palace. There is that worthy part which, being set free, is free to express itself in the fullness of God and His presence. It is almost like releasing the fish from the pond or bowl into the immensity of the sea, there to find its own place among those of kindred nature.

When a teacher takes hold of a piece of chalk, that chalk is set free on the largeness of the blackboard. The same applies with the pen in the hand as it is placed onto the sheet of paper. In that which it is made part of and placed upon it finds its total fulfilment. Heaven and Eternity to you is that you might finally be fully yourself, the self that God has created you to be. As every flower needs space in a garden, so in God there is that which we require to express our maturity. What a waste when a person so developed in God wastes that maturity. God took a man, walked with that man and matured that man — Enoch. His experience and description of continuing life is found in Genesis 5:18–24, Hebrews 11:5 and Jude verse 14.

God chooses His own time and place

When the time was right and the wine within him was mature, God took Enoch to be with Himself. Not because His purposes for that life were finished, but because God had some new purposes to fulfil. Larger promises need a larger place for fulfilment. That is why we need the Heavenly sphere, the travelling in another direction. What God did with Enoch, the man whose name means 'initiated' or 'dedicated', He is seeking to do with you, until you take your flight to worlds unknown. Dedicated on earth, to be initiated into the unknown of glory. That which is mystery for you can become majestic. Enoch leaves a pathway right into the palace of gold. He became the gateway to God, proving that dying is living.

Enoch is one of two men who never saw death. Elijah was the other. Genesis 5:18–24, Hebrews 11:5 and Jude 14 all tell how Enoch passed through the veil of death without dying. He passed through death intact in the life that God had granted him. Death is described in the phrase 'God took him'. Death for you can be God acting on your behalf as promised in the New Testament through Jesus Christ, who wanted us to be where He is[1]. Forever with the Lord[2] is a New Testament phrase, fulfilled in Enoch, describing the way he passed from this life into a deeper, fuller expansion of existence. There came a decided and decisive moment of his departure. He didn't come to a brick wall, a precipice or a dark wood. God took him. Come to My place! What had been the fellowship of light was made even brighter in death. God called him in!

Death cannot be more simple or more profound than that. Dying for you, even as Enoch, can be God taking His treasure to be within His treasure chest. We call it death. God calls it Life. We refer to the end, God speaks of it as a beginning. The pearl had found its place. That which is part of God is taken by God into His bosom to be hugged and loved forever in life. God robs death and the grave on your behalf. He closes down cemeteries, locking the gates for ever, breaking the flowers which make the wreaths by this simple act of love. To walk with God and then not to be found — God gets the blame!

Enoch is placed right at the beginning of the Old Testament to give hope to all who follow. We are among those who follow in his footsteps because his God is our God, made more friendly in Jesus. If the love of God leads to anything it leads to this thing for you, life before death, through death and after death. It is life, the life of God which is stronger and beyond death. The hand of God is seen beyond its scope. Enoch was not, for God took him but God ever was and ever shall be. There is more than you can see. More stars than you can count. More blue sky than enters the circle of the eye.

God acts independently of natural life

As to Enoch's body and what God did when he was translated we are not told. In Revelation 11:3 there are those who tell us that these two 'witnesses' are Enoch and Elijah, the two Old Testament men who never died. If that is true it means that the Almighty has something more after we have passed into the beyond. That which we do not know, God knows. When things of time and sense disappear, God appears as He always has been. What a comfort! What a joy! We are still the messengers of God, still His servants, still hand in hand with our God.

The fellowship lasts into and throughout Eternity. There is deep union here, a deep mine of fellowship, a finality which isn't final at all. The final whistle is never blown. Darkness never brings the day to an end. It never will for those with faith in the living God. The sun rises to set no more. The independence of the nature of God is seen more clearly in death than in any other act. He never dies. You cannot bury Him with a spade. Atheism has tried many times with its blunt shovel!

1 Thessalonians 4:15–18 informs and describes, as does 1 Corinthians 15, what will happen, not only at our death but also at the rapture and the resurrection of believers. God will fulfil all through Jesus Christ. He is the Person and the promise of the resurrection. He is the power of that resurrection, the provision of resurrection.

God has promised future life

Each type, each simple ceremony is given for our admonition and learning. When we open the Bible we are gazing at God's map of the future world. We learn about living and dying through the life of Enoch. What has happened once for him can happen and does happen again for you as promised by the Son of God.[3] Some who are alive will be translated even as Enoch was. Seeds are sown in Scripture and those sown through this patriarch become part of the promises of God to you. If God has done it for one, He can do it for everyone. If Jesus can raise Lazarus from the dead then He can raise everyone from the dead! Practice results in performance!

Hebrews 11:5, King James version, mentions Enoch's translation three times, and the emphasis is not on the dying but places wisdom, hope and knowledge into those things we do not understand. It is an unbroken, threefold cord and it is the finest epitaph ever written for mankind. Not dead, not gone, not decomposing, but demonstrating future existence. Written, never to fade with time, singing songs with the angels, not to corruption but to Christ and resurrection!

There has to be a place to where God can take Enoch. Heaven — the home of the free. It is your other home, your summer house, the destination which never comes to a stop. We are never sent into the sidings, we never come to the place where we can go no further. If God takes us, then there is so much more beyond, as large as He is. The love of God is multicoloured, embracing all who come to Him. The emphasis is not on the simple taking of a body, it is a translation which gives meaning, as when a foreign language is translated. A dead language becomes a living language! What happened gives meaning, not only translation but interpretation. There was nothing foreign, nothing that required interpretation. It is not a glass darkly, as spoken of by the writer to the Corinthian Church[4]. It is plainer than the day.

God made a way for Enoch to enter His presence

Enoch broke the curse placed on mankind, the curse of death.[5] Instead of going down, he went up. Instead of stopping, he went further. There was no disappearing into dust, it was a passing on with the Divine. This translation is seen in emigration and migration. The body will be different. We die as we live. We end as we began. A good life will give great confidence in death. Death is an extension of what we have been. It is not simply transportation but translation, not just a change of view.

Enoch did not have to take his pains and aches with him. It was to a whole new destination in God. There had been no hope, just the clay, the coffin, yet now he rises through God to new heights. The God who took him could and would transform him. Hell will be transport provided but without the translation into God's Kingdom, creation without satisfaction, an end in itself. Heaven is but a beginning, never ending, a continuation of the transforming power of God. If you could take your healthiest and happiest moments and have them forever without change, decay, pain or hurt, weariness or tiredness, that would be Heaven.

Jude 14 prophesied the coming of the Lord. Did he do it through his life and lip, what he said and how he lived for God? Enoch, a figure from Scripture, was very much involved in the death of all those who love the Lord.

God was pleased with Enoch

Hebrews 11:5 says he pleased God. He pleased God with his life, his love, his walk and his talk. The aroma of an earthly life was scent to Heaven's scene. Saintly steps led upwards and onwards. This is the way for you to live and will be the way for you to die. The tree that is rooted deep and firm will have a branch that takes fruit over the wall into another world. The facts of faith were there, spread into and around his life. It was faith which told him to live for God now, because there was life after death, a dawn after the darkness and a light at the end of the tunnel. The teaching hand was something to reach for. The loving heart has a future to love and live for.

There is a golden hope for you found in the golden streets of Heaven, beyond the setting sun and the rising moon. It is faith which prepares in order for God to introduce you to His world. God closes the door of one world as He opens the door to the other. Each person has the opportunity of an Eternity with God. That has to be blessed! There is a future inbuilt within faith. Part of the pleasure of pleasing God was to be taken into another world. Enoch took God into his own home and God, in return, took Enoch into His, to the place where nothing comes to an end. There are new beginnings everyday for you in your Eternity. What great things God has wrought! Part of walking with God is heaven. The next best thing to loving God, is Heaven.

God came down into our world

There was a world that Jesus Christ in His incarnation came into, as there is a world above into which we will go. He became one of us that He might reach us. He came unto His own, they received Him not. He came unto and into the unknown and they received Him.

Often you have been as the water beetle, living in the dark muddy pond with stones at the bottom, old shoes and prams, bits of wrecks surrounding you. One day you rise to the surface. What sights and what sounds! How can they be described? How could Enoch describe what happened to him when God took him? I like that, don't you — Good took him? It doesn't say how far or where to, it is not measured or monitored. For God to take you up at death when all men can do is place you down in a hole is wonderful indeed!

God has prepared delightful things for us

I was raised near a coal mine in South Yorkshire, England. Every summer there was an exit of the pit ponies into the green fields beyond the mine. Those horses were delighted when they savoured the smell of the open field after the dark mine. Their hooves seemed to gather thunder! What a task we had to coax them back into the mines to pull the wagons! They had seen and known better things.

You may feel that you are in that blackness, but there are green pastures and waters of quietness of Psalm 23 ahead. (See author's book.) I will dwell in the house of the Lord forever. Not a shack or a tent but a house. The pleasure became a pathway into the Heavenlies. God took Enoch as you might take a flower or a cup of water to your lips. That which was held dear was held near. Life after death is all about you finding your place in God's house, even as the sun, moon and stars find their place in the sky. Eternity is big, but God is bigger. In the unknown there is the known. I shall be known as I am known.

God disciplines through life and in life

Enoch means 'dedicated'. That which you have given yourself to, that you will possess. It suggests a narrow walk. It means discipleship and holiness. Those who are going to a different world must be different. Enoch was walking with God and they were going somewhere together. Discipleship, even at death, is ongoing. Fanny Crosby, the blind hymnwriter expresses life after death in her hymn:

> 'Ever He walks beside me,
> Brightly His sunshine appears
> Spreading a beautiful rainbow,
> Over a valley of tears.'

It does not stop when you cease to breathe. The principles are as eternal as the hills, the summers of a lifetime. He left us not only a testimony about death but also about life, how to live and how to die, how to pass through death and stay alive. He lived on in the form of God, in what God had provided for him. God has prepared some lovely things for those who love Him[6].

A walk with God will result in being in His presence. His footprints did not cease on earth. Your footprints will not lead to a grave. They may cease at that grave to the natural eye, but your feet will walk on as a pilgrim bound for a city. Beyond the grave is a goal. We are going to the city of refuge. What Enoch was continued. He was a pleaser of God. Goodness and mercy never die. They travel on, character marks set as the sun to rise again in another world in deeper splendour. A pool of dirty water is raised into the atmosphere by the sun and appears as part of a rainbow. This is your life!

God wants those who will walk with Him

Enoch was wide awake even in death. He had no time to change things or put his house in order. Enoch walked with God before he passed through death into life with God. The very nature of God wrapped itself around him, introducing a change where there had been only change and decay. God, the unchangeable element; God, the ongoing purpose; God, the unshakeable Rock. With God all things are possible. This is not beyond belief, it is belief in the beyond, even as I believe that there is a whole world in the pond at the bottom of my garden.

With God all things unseen are. The things that are not yours yet, shall be. There were things alive before you came into existence and there are things in existence beyond. Death is but the lifting of the veil, the frown before the smile. It is the doubt of the passenger who has never previously flown or sailed, yet on arrival at the destination wonders at the doubt. Death, here in Enoch, is defined as 'a walk with God'. It isn't hitch hiking with thumb, but His hand crucified. It is being carried.

Dying is going on in God

The child said to his friend, who had noticed that the goldfish bowl was empty: 'The goldfish has gone to God.' It was the child's way of expressing death. There is something real for the reader of these pages! There is proof! Luke refers to them as 'many infallible proofs'[7].

There is a better and a brighter tomorrow for every believer. All your yesterdays and all your todays will be part of a new tomorrow. Something of every day, lived by Enoch, was carried with him. You are the flame of the Lord and must appear as light in the Lord. There are many phrases connected with the words 'with the Lord'. 1 Thessalonians 4:18, 'forever with the Lord'. In the hand, in the mind, in the presence, in the circle of His crown of gold. The very centre of all that God is will be for your comfort and cherishing.

Enoch, before his rapture, pleased God. He was a pleasure to God, as much a pleasure as the six days of wonderful creation. It will take longer to develop character in you. He was as much a pleasure as the offering of Abel. What is a pleasure to you, Enoch was to God. He pleased God. The word 'pleasing' is the normal word for a servant pleasing his master. As used in the Septuagint versions of the Old Testament it is found in

Hebrews 13:16, and reveals the aroma and the sacrifice of his life. He pleased God here and God was to please him in Heaven. The bee which collects the honey also pollinates the flowers. The life of blessing is the blessed life. The beauty of life and nature given to Enoch was given back to God for God to take and further it. The faded of earth became the fulness of Heaven.

God grants the assurance of life beyond

To walk up and on, to go in and through, to come out at the other side, he had to walk in step with God, to have a line of communication. He had the conviction that there was another side to living, and it was not death. There was another side to the mountain. Wait until you see the other side! There is another side to life. We have only known the dark side. We have very often lived on the wrong side of the cloud, we have never seen the silver lining. The clouds will be parted by a rainbow, magnificent colours displayed in and through you.

'Walked with God' contains the idea of persistence and progress. The name Enoch can also mean educated or trained. Life is all about being trained for Heaven. Earth is God's royal school, for royal children, and He will have no illiterate people in His school. This life is an education, not of the mind but of that part that will go through death and into life. We are receiving things here and now to be revealed there and then.

Education is more than books and learning, it is going through, reaching the other side of the hill. Houses destroyed always seem to be far better when they are rebuilt. There is that described as better and then there is the best! As Browning said, 'The best is yet to be.'

God lives with us hourly, daily and for ever

It is easy to live for God for a week, but turn the hours into days and the days into weeks and months. It is a long time to carry the cross. It is easier to believe that your friend is going to give you a gift when the five pound note is in your hand, rather than in his pocket! There is that which will be given by God, but not yet.

Enoch's whole life was spent in getting to know God. When the time came to meet Him, he had no need to ask who are you? Like those in

John 21:7, who having spent three and a half years with Jesus, he was able to say, 'It is the Lord.' Jesus was waiting on the shore. What a picture of your arrival in Heaven. There are distinctions to be learned. Our trials help us to distinguish God for the things around us, help us to separate God from time and friends. All we are left with is God.

Every step and every day God was preparing Enoch for the translation. Training, ready for the taking. There was the God element surrounding him day by day. We are never told that he stopped walking with God.

God is there at the beginning and at the continuing of life

Enoch's faith reached out and took that which would help him. Uneven ground on earth becomes gold streets in Heaven. Faith gives eyes which see Heaven as if it is on your doorstep as readily available as the daily milk. It grants telescopic and microscopic views of life.

Walking describes Enoch's whole manner of life. It was not simply putting his shoes on, taking a few steps. All the steps he ever took are meaningful. Everything he did or said was in that walking. The best walk was not among the trees or flowers, by the river or in the local park, but with God. Walk not only with the pleasurable but with the Immeasurable. God was the whole tenor of his life. When God means so much to you, Heaven sparkles in your eyes.

God walks with us through life into eternity

To walk you need a way and a destination. Every sailing ship has a port. The King's Highway was to be walked upon. God was Enoch's signpost. The way we walk, what we do and what we are depends with whom we are walking. It says of Jesus, 'They beheld His walk.'[8]

Do you walk as a person who is going somewhere? Is there a light beyond your dark tunnel that you are going towards? There was a Church in Yorkshire, England, where a whole group of Christians lived in the houses on the same street and it became known locally as 'Hallelujah Avenue!'

Because he was walking with God, every trial was passed through, every hill and mountain, valley and plateau was passed. Every walk in faith can be a walk in the park. It will probably kill you to get there! The earth didn't suddenly open up, but God did and the walker entered in. The Rock split. What happened to Enoch will happen to us. Colossians 1:13 says 'We have been translated from the kingdom of darkness into Light.' It means to be carried away. We have been carried out of sin and into salvation so then there is to be another carrying away from this world into Heaven. The mighty power of God will accomplish it all.

God has arranged the Rapture through Jesus

In referring to the second coming of Jesus Christ and the Rapture, which may happen even before you surrender your body to God in death, 1 Thessalonians 4:17 says we shall be 'caught up'. It is a very strong word. The word is 'rape', so sudden, just as rape can be. The Latin is 'repare', to snatch. A man snatches a woman's handbag; a thief snatches the wages; a child snatches an apple. All these are pictures of translation and Rapture. The man who fell among thieves on the Jericho Road was robbed. It means to be as sudden as that, without any warning.

Enoch was not only translated, he was transparent and transportable. He was Raptured. Much of his translation took place on earth as he walked with God, but as he was taken there had to be that change. Anyone looking for him had to look for God. We are going to be quickened.

God cares and carries us forward

Enoch, it says, was translated, Genesis 5:24, Hebrews 11:5. The word is used in the Septuagint version of the Bible in Acts 7:15–17 where it describes the bones of Jacob being carried from one place to another. Joseph was raptured but not changed in a moment, in the twinkling of an eye.

A little boy illustrated what he thought was meant by the term 'in the twinkling of an eye' by winking at his father. 'As quick as that, Dad?' he asked. Galatians 1:6 describes the sudden change of attitude of the Galatian believers. Hebrews 7:12, of a change of priesthood.

To be rapturous is when you are suddenly lifted up. I sing in my rapture. The sudden upsurge of inspiration. The lifting of your spirit, the introduction of another mood.

You translate when copying one language into another. There are many Bible translations, many Bible translators. It is the placing of Hebrew, Greek and Aramaic into English. Translated is to put over into another place, to transfer to another place. I have taken funds from my current account and have deposited them in my savings account. To go to one place from another. All this will happen when Jesus comes as He went, in like manner[9].

God will do His translating work according to His Word

Translated, 1 Corinthians 13:2, is the word used to describe the casting of mountains, the removing of them. In our English language the word is 'metathesis' referring to the transposition of a letter or word. It is to have it all arranged as if it has been a pile of children's bricks, marked with different letters, placed into a perfect word and sentence. It means to spell correctly, to correct the error. Many speak with doubt at the very heart of their words. You yourself may have doubt-centre words in relation to life after death. Yours may be a stuttering tongue when expressing your faith in the resurrection. God has expressed this truth in full oratory.

Philippians 3:21 needs to be added to your translation from one place to another. Enoch was changed, but by God. His faith in God made it all possible. God is the architect and the builder and He certainly will bring it to pass. Blessed are the homesick, for, at last, they shall come to the Father's House.

When some books are translated into foreign languages there is a requirement for more than one translator because some are more expert at rendering moods and pictures into appropriate words. God is the best translator of all! He does with lives what others only do with words. God changes all that we are and have into the best possible use and it becomes true beauty in His hands.

God makes all things new, including you

When Charles I, King of England, died, a little mongrel dog followed the bier containing his body. On its collar were the words: 'I am Caesar and I belong to the King.'

D.L. Moody, a famous Evangelist of the last Century wrote in the margin of his Bible: 'If God is your partner, make your plans big.'

The skies, not the grave is our goal. Your destiny is not in your immediate locality. The God who provides the stuff and the staff of life will also provide the serenity of everlasting life.

God takes us home in mercy while men bury us in pity

An atheist was dying and was heard to whisper in his fear, 'I am leaving home.' A Christian lady in the same town was also dying. She was heard to say with great conviction: 'I am going home! I am going home!' Yet another Christian was heard to utter the words to an unseen Presence: 'I am coming home.' To the Red Indians of America it was to go where the river does not bend, the waters do not disappear, where the grass remains green forever. You have heard of an Indian Summer!

In the Outer Hebrides, Scotland, there is a legend of a god who lives in the sea. They have a special name for him. This god longed to have a baby of his own. He was always seeking to catch one, to take it away into the sea with him. Mothers kept their children very close to them but one day a child was washed over by a wave. As the wave withdrew with the sea the child was heard to say: 'One day he will return for me, for part of me is in his heart and part of him has entered into my heart through that wave.' So the child grew and became a young man. One day he took a boat out to sea and was never seen again. The god who had become part of him had called and collected him!

Enoch became the firstfruit of those who have gone before in the early part of Creation. He has blazed a trail to include you, and left footprints for you to follow, footsteps right to the throne of God, into the heart of God.

Commencing where he commenced, we shall conclude where he entered into the full and complete care of God. Eternity to God is but a circle with His love in the middle and in every part of that circle. To Enoch, dying was living. It was the opportunity to be free. The caged bird was set free to sing in the four corners of the world. The shackles of sense and time were snapped, the prison doors opened and Enoch stepped out of time and into the timeless zone of God, from human limitations into the limitless dimension of that called Divine life.

NOTES

1. John 17:24.
2. 1 Thessalonians 4:17.
3. 1 Thessalonians 5:10; Hebrews 11:5.
4. 1 Corinthians 13:12.
5. Genesis 3:19.
6. 1 Corinthians 2:9.
7. Acts 1:3.
8. John 1:36.
9. Acts 1:11.

Shall We Recognise Friends in the Life Beyond?

There are many who wonder, as the body of a loved one is gently lowered into the grave, Shall I ever see them again? Will they ever recognise me? Will we know loved ones in the future life? That firm handshake, the knowing smile, the gentle touch, the easy gait — will I recognise it again? There is an answer.

Shall we attribute to a perfect body, perfect knowledge and wisdom, less than we know now? Shall we have less intelligence than we have had on earth? Through our dismayed eyes and feeble frames we have recognised people during this life, indeed life has been very much an identification parade and we have witnessed so many things. The answer surely is that we shall be known as we are known[1].

There will be recognition of others

Recognition is not just a matter of recognising shape or physical form. Some people are known by the sound of their voice. I once prayed in a large conference, and my voice was recognised by one person at the back of an auditorium where thousands were present. The voice, as the body, has a certain distinction. All lighthouses have a different light; each bee has a distinctive sound; each chime of every Church bell is different. You may receive a message without a signature but you know who it is from. There is recognition by calligraphy. No-one writes, spells or expresses themselves as you do. A young girl sent a card to her blind father. She wrote no words but simply sprayed her perfume onto the clean white card.

A lack of hair, a tear or sob marks people out for recognition without the need to see them physically. We recognise them by a thousand different ways. Forensic science tells us that we all leave evidences of where we have been and can be recognised by those tell-tale marks. We have an individual DNA makeup and this is one of the sure proofs against evolution. Gathering all the evidence together can determine who the person is. There will be many things in the future life that will add up to the person you have known and loved. Neither deep love or real friendship can ever be dissolved. It can never die in a grave but will live on in grace.

Many were recognised after death

In the Gospels the people recognised Moses and Elijah.[2] This was because of their appearance. They lived on after death. When Jesus mentioned some who had died they were still known by name. 'Lazarus, come forth!' 'Tabitha,' Peter said, 'Arise.' The disciples did not recognise Jesus on the Emmaus Road, in Luke 24, because their eyes were holden — held shut.[3] Usually, like Mary after the resurrection they recognised Jesus Christ. There was something about His voice, the way He said, 'Mary.' Such tender notes. They knew it was the Lord when He appeared to His followers in John 21. Thomas, doubting Thomas, when he was invited to reach forth his finger and place it in the side and hands knew it was Jesus. There he buried all his unbelief forever. When Jesus suddenly appeared in the midst of the disciples they knew Him. God has a million ways for you to recognise those who have passed from this life into the next.

We will recognise and remember

Jesus told a story of a man who recognised those in the future life, and remembered those in past life, in Luke 16:19–31. All the faculties of the body are presented to us in a person who has died. He has touch, feeling, compassion, understanding. The rich man has the same features, he feels pain, he knows fully and understands fully. The scent of the rose, whether in the flower or inside a bottle, is still scent.

There are those who would expound that Luke 16:19–31 is just a parable, yet unlike any other parable, names are mentioned. If it is a parable — as if that makes it a lesser truth — then what is the teaching to be received from this pulpit? If you accept one part of it as true, then you must accept all of it. This Heavenly story must not be denied Heavenly meaning. The Word of God stands or falls by this premise — it is all or nothing. If the first part of the story of angels and Abraham's bosom is true, then the torment part of the same story must also be true. The recognition of the rich man Lazarus must be authentic, the knowledge and memory faculty accepted. One has to admit that there is no other portion of Scripture like it. It is a window into the after life. If you apply all the laws of parable and earthly story with Heavenly meaning you are still left with the teaching of Jesus on life after death. There is a naming of names, a circle of recognition.

The Jewish faith taught recognition after death

The phrase 'Abraham's bosom' was proverbial, but also real. It is exactly what the Jews believed and received as part of their teaching from an early age, and that teaching was confirmed in Jesus. He took it and placed it in the heart of Christianity, using it to explain what happens on the other side of the grave. The known always breaks the power of the unknown. That which is conceived cancels out that which is concealed. Jesus used words in picture form, giving recognition and the facts of future life through those words.

Who else but Jesus could throw back the dark curtain separating time from Eternity and show recognition in action? Lazarus did not have to ask who Abraham was. There was recognition as immediate as the leaving of the body, and being lifted by angels into Abraham's bosom. Angels knew Abraham and they knew the beggar also. They knew the place where they had to convey him.

The beggar died, but was not buried. There is no soul sleep. The real part of him, the living remaining existence was taken to a place of retreat and recollection. There was more beyond.

There will be knowing and being known

The angels calling to collect was only part of the programme. There is an immediate absence from the body and presence with the Lord. He was carried by the angels into Abraham's bosom. There is something so gentle, so soft and beautiful, words of hope and comfort better than flowers. The best bouquets fade away but this scene remains forever. If it is a parable at all, it must be a parable of the recognition of familiar things after death, a parable of friends beyond the grave, known and knowing one another.

It is unfortunate that the word 'hell' appears in Luke 16:23. It is not the Gehenna, the lake of fire or torment, as in Revelation 19:20; 20:10,14, but the world of the unseen where departed spirits go at death, the unknown and the unseen world, as viewed from this life. Yet there is a light in that darkness, presented by Jesus Christ. Every word is a beaming ray of light. Some would cut it, as with a knife, separate it into two areas. Lazarus went to where Abraham had his seat. Kings had their seat of residence and power. Lazarus recognised Abraham as the great rescuer from death, even as he had been with his nephew Lot.[4]

Abraham was so great in faith that even after death people came to him for comfort and help. His earthly ministry extended into Eternity. Lazarus required no formal introduction. What was good enough for angels was good enough for him. We can go from living in Jesus to resting with Abraham, part and parcel of all that faith can grant to us. When we die we go to the fountain head of all faith. As believers we are the children of Abraham.[5]

Lazarus was carried, borne along by angels to the heart of Abraham as wine is to the lips. There is a well known figure in the cloudless beyond — we shall never be totally alone. It is as large as it is deep, as wide as it is welcoming. There was recognition of fire, flame, torments and tongues.

Wordsworth refers to being in Abraham's bosom in 'It is a Beauteous Evening'. William Shakespeare, in *King Richard The Third*, tells of those who sleep in Abraham's bosom. There is a suggestion of tranquillity, to be at home and to be at one with your pioneer. When earth leaves us, Abraham takes over. I can leave the working out of my future with faithful Abraham!

There will be those we readily respond to

Abraham's bosom throws up many suggestions. To the Jew it was the very heart of the universe. For the Christian it suggests repose in faith, meaning a returning to the very fountain head — back to the original principle, to be with our role model, back to the beginning where there is a man of faith in the future. Lazarus had no complaints. In Eternity you will be with those who are like you. Lazarus became part of the circle of friends.

One definition of a friend is a leafy tree. Lazarus had a contribution to make, not what he could get, but what he could give. As a beggar others had given to him all his life, now, for the first time ever, he could give something. He was more than a bundle of rags, he was an acknowledged person.

After this life has ceased we shall be as those in John 21:4, where it says, 'and it was morning'. This time of the day speaks of identification. We recognise the things around us by the morning light. Jesus stood on the shore and after a little discussion with the others Peter said, 'It is the Lord.' By a fire He fed them, from the old burned out ashes there came a new fellowship and realisation of who Jesus Christ was. Part of His ministry was recognition. We shall not be lost and ignorant in Eternity, all things are known by Him.

There will be many aspects of recognition

All the characteristics of the body are found in the rich man. He sees, he knows, he smells, he has a memory, he is tormented — all speak of recognition. Things that we so readily recognise in this life are recognised in the future also. The pain is wiped away but there are memories. It satisfies Lazarus, him whom God helps, to remain just where he is.

Another Lazarus, the brother of Mary and Martha, was called from the bosom of Abraham to the bosom of Jesus.[6] The bosom is a step on the way to eternal destiny, an oasis by the way. It will be resting on the bosom until we say, 'Jesus, Lover of my soul, let me to Thy Bosom fly.' As Charles Wesley stood by an open window he saw a hawk chasing a smaller bird. The bird flew in through the open window into the bosom or chest of Charles Wesley and because of this incident he wrote the well known hymn. Lazarus in Abraham's bosom has come to the end of a journey, the end of sores and suffering. He is not cast outside the door but is inside, in Abraham's bosom.

Paul says it is far better.[7] It is better than the best, whatever best you have at this moment. You cannot top the top! God's care did not cease in this life. The hand was not empty or closed into a fist to threaten with, it was still full of helpful things given to him in this new dispensation. The best wine was set forth at the last. We shall meet Abraham, as any father would meet with his family. From the north, south, east and west they will be seated in the Kingdom with Abraham, and with Jacob. The best is yet to be. Lazarus is near the heart of this Father of the faithful.

The rich man can never feel the throb of the thing very near to him. He recognises the emptiness and the futility of life. He loses everything, not because he was rich but because there was no trust, no faith element in his life. His true riches were in poverty when his garments were rags. He was not a follower of Faithful Father Abraham. Care for others came too late.

There is refuge and restful recognition

The word 'bosom' can mean a bay, a gulf, where ships go during or after a storm, a haven on the edge of a rough sea. It is the place of refuge for birds when the winds are too strong.

There were two gulfs in this story, one fixed, the other soft, yielding and warm, as the inside of a bird's nest. One as a great wide space, the other as the heart of Father Abraham. The word bosom or bay can mean a pocket. In that pocket of God is all you will ever need. It is used as a figure of paying liberally, or can mean the area inside the girdle which was used for keeping precious things, drawn up and tucked in around the middle. You matter to Him, you are His jewels, recognised by God. Security and safety is here.

Jeremy Taylor, an early commentator, translates Abraham's bosom as 'The Bay of Abraham', the place to which ships came after a long voyage — the English Falmouth or Scarborough Bay, bringing ships to familiar surroundings and friends. The ship has travelled the seas, braved the storms, successfully carried its cargo to its destination and now reached the unloading bay, the place of tranquility and surety. The child comes to the breast of the Mother for comfort and so finds recognition, love and warmth.

This recognition is richer and deeper than that which is on earth

Some scholars suggest that the bosom of Abraham is synonymous with Paradise, to be where the faith aspect takes us. It means that we enter into a loving relationship and fellowship at death. Your faith will lead you to the Father of the faithful. Be assured, reader, faith is leading somewhere and to someone.

John 13:23; 21:20 describes the old Roman and Jewish banquet, of reclining at a meal where the head rested on the bosom or near to the chest of another. The beloved disciple rested his head on the breast of Jesus.[8] There was such closeness and recognition. Appreciation had a feast of its own. Warmth filled each cup. The bosom is a hollow thing but in its depths is found such power. Power to give sight and understanding, power to heal every hurt, power to help you understand it all.

> 'We'll talk it over in the bye and bye,
> We'll talk it over, my Lord and I,
> I'll ask the reason, He'll tell me why,
> We'll talk it over in the bye and bye.'[9]

There will be the fellowship of recognition

It suggests to be in immediate fellowship with another. There is no fellowship without the intimacy of knowledge and recognition. It is the area of firsthand information. It will be the reclining, just as the disciples did in the Upper Room, of the righteous, where they knew each other by name and so shall we. Questions were asked, answers given, plans presented and discussed, a course of action decided upon.

Matthew 8:11; Luke 13:28,29; 14:16; all describe the banquet or feast where the most favoured guest was offered the position nearest to the master of the house, the highest position. The highest, widest and deepest association awaits you among those whom you will recognise and it will be a mutual recognition.

It can be the picture of the lamb as it is carried away from the wolf, darkness and fear, carried across the chest of the shepherd. The lamb knows the shepherd, he is a familiar friend. There is nothing distant or cold about this scene of the bosom. The shepherd wants to put warmth back into the lamb after the freezing conditions. The days of the unknown have ceased, the sheep is no longer on the dusty path it is in the fold, resting on the bosom of the shepherd whose body is laid across the doorway for safety. That knowledge in part, seeing through some glass darkly, is complete, because that which is perfect has come.

The harvest was gathered into the bosom. Large gifts placed there as thanks are given. If we only had the hope of recognising people in this life, then of all men we would be the most miserable. Eternity with limited knowledge of friends would be imperfect. Both recognised Abraham, they understood each other.

John 1:18, Jesus is depicted as being in the bosom of the Father. He declared the Father because He knew that Father. It is to have the deepest of fellowship and nearness, to be in touch. We have the warmth of another's love and presence very near to us. The future is opened as a tranquil scene of rest and peace, no armies, no shout and bark, no gun or bomb. This is truly Psalm 23 in a condensed form, 'I will fear no evil for you are with me.' In the original language there is no 'are with'. It should read — You, Me. Nothing in between.

There is no fighting or worry, just calm repose and recognition of all that has been provided. You will enter into it as a new baby enters into that which has been readily provided. For those who have gone before and those who will join them, the future is assured. This story has become the circle of certainty. Everyone is rested and conversing. It is what Abraham did for his earthly visitors before the promised child Isaac was mentioned[10].

It is a picture of the King's feast on returning from battle. All his outstanding men of ability are known and shown but do they know the King? It is where the instrument, after much practice, is retuned.

Lazarus had a name whilst the rich man did not. What earth could never give to him was given and granted by the future world. He was ushered into the same dispensation and age as Abraham. They still talk, feel, listen and love. They can still appreciate good things. Your love will widen the circle.

There will be the peace and depth of recognition

Abraham's bosom means the pouch[11]. It was above the girdle which was made by pulling up the garment slightly. It may refer to the care of a mother who gathers her child in the folds of her upper dress and near to her bosom. It was the place of milk, food and drink, sustenance and joy, the very fountain of life.

The Jews often presented life after death as some feast. They expected to be welcomed by Abraham. They felt, rightly, that there would be someone they would recognise first, and they would know earth's familiar friends. This same Father of the faithful has greater acceptance, is the very source of the faith of every believer. We shall be where he is, not above and not below. Many will be there, but best of all, you will be there, in the same place, enjoying the same style of living. Angels fly to Abraham as tame birds come to the hand to be fed. The mind and the heart in a perfect state needs no training.

A Rabbi, Adda Bar Ahab uses this same expression of one departed into the after life. Abraham's bosom is not simply a Jewish concept of death, it is part of Jesus' theology and eschatology, which we can receive and believe. One who comes from beyond to tell us the secrets of after life. Here is the tour guide, the brochure of the blessed! To be absent from the body is to be present with the Lord. That is where Abraham was.

Canon Girdlestone, writing in *Old Testament Synonyms* puts it succinctly when he speaks of one of the names given to God, Shaddai, which means the Almighty. 'The word is connected with a root which means breast. The many breasted God, speaking of His fullness and exhuberance.' Abraham has a many breasted God, and when we die there is a breast to go to, as a child would go to its mother's breast to rest in comfort and peace. Bishop Ryle states, 'It was probably an accepted proverb, but it is fully fulfilled in the life of this one who had little recognition.'

There is an intermediate state. There is a location to which all believers go. From the kick, push and shove to the quietness of a bosom. From being unknown to being known, unrecognised to recognised. In 1 Samuel 17:56, after David had slayed Goliath, Saul makes the enquiry, 'Whose stripling is this young man?'

John Gill, the Puritan writer, says, 'The term Abraham's bosom was well known to the Jews. It was part of Jewish thought, a phrase through which they expressed future happiness. They had no doubt of the happiness of Abraham and when they died they were to share it with him. "He sits in the bosom of Abraham. He has gone to Abraham's bosom. He is safe and sound".' Matthew 8:11,12 says to sit in the Kingdom was a feast. You reposed with Abraham, Isaac and Jacob. Here is a more remarkable thing — those you have not seen, known or heard of in the past, now, because of the perfect environment, you will know. You will recognise them! Peter, John, Moses, Abraham, Noah!

Your greatest appreciation will be reserved for Jesus Christ. They shall see His face. It is the look of knowing and recognising, not a stare into a blank space. We shall know all others because we shall know Him. Not one will say in the Eternity stretching before you, 'Who are you, Lord?'

There will be the recognition of child and parent

The beggar had a realisation of father Abraham and Abraham recognised brother Lazarus. John Trapp writes, 'It is said by some that it describes children when they have been running and knock themselves and then come to mother for comfort.' They recognise and know from past experience all the comfort, all the love of mother. There is the suggestion of freedom from pain. There is the welcome by the one who is familiar.

Matthew Henry says, 'The Jews expressed death in three ways: they go to the Garden of Eden; they go under the throne of glory; they go to Abraham's bosom.' It is soft, clean, yielding, moulded to the form and there is perfect peace. Abraham has been the father of multitudes and as such his faith has satisfied endless multitudes. His bosom is large enough to sustain all who rest there in faith. Of all who have come to rest on the bosom of Jesus, the saintly Rutherford, the Scottish divine, used to say, 'There is still room for one more.' There was nothing ornate, this is a resting place, awaiting the new body of Resurrection and final Heaven.

If we are going to Abraham's bosom then we must live as Abraham did. We must be his other half, his shadow, his brother, his son, each must be an Isaac, meaning 'laughter'. Every person in the position of laughter in Abraham's place, is God's laugh at the devil. Oh, the joy and laughter that fills our very being when we realise that we will be among recognised and recognisable friends. The circle will not be broken, but completed as you arrive with your unique contribution. We must be the very substance of the One we are going to be with. We must take to Him what is most like Him — that which is produced by faith and by being the friend of God. The friends of God will gather with the friend of God. Each person there will be able to say of each other what God said of Abraham, 'I know him...'[12].

NOTES

1. 1 Corinthians 13:12.
2. Matthew 17:3,4.
3. Luke 24:16.
4. Genesis 14.
5. Galatians 3:7.
6. John 11:43.
7. Philippians 1:23.
8. John 13:23.
9. A well known spiritual song.
10. Genesis 18:7,8.
11. *Dictionary of New Testament Theology*, edited by Colin Brown. Volume 1, published by Paternoster Press.
12. Genesis 18:19.

12

What Will the New Resurrection Body Be Like?

Wﾀe have noted earlier that Paul's departure was at hand. Now we come to discover what the writer/believer expected when he moved from this scene, when he stepped out of this body. He was being prepared for a future existence in the presence of God. Your preparation is neither more nor less than his. The same carpenter who worked on Paul has been at work in your life through the Holy Spirit. The same builder has been laying foundation stones in truths which you have received.

The new resurrection body

Moffatt's rendering of 2 Corinthians 5:1 is, 'If this earthly tent of mine is taken down I get a home from God.' If we are going to have a body, and Jesus will bring us back as a people with a body, we have to establish, from 1 Corinthians 15:35, with what body do they come? Some in the Corinthian Church were asking the same sort of questions that we ask. The Corinthians needed a lot of persuasion and illustration. Some were even baptised for the dead,[1] thinking that those who died in Jesus were lost forever. They wanted to know as they would be known. The broken picture or the dark glass[2] was not enough. They wanted to know what body there would be in the future. The gaze into the riddle solved nothing. They wanted it in black and white, and in pink and yellow if possible, and sealed with seven seals within and without!

The nature of the new body

Paul answers this in 1 Corinthians 15:35–45. There are bodies of wheat, maize, oats, flowers, bulbs, fish, birds, bodies terrestrial and celestial, sun, moon, and stars. There are buildings of brick and steel, wood, clay, coral, vegetation and fibre. Even heads on bodies, feet, hands and arms are shaped differently. God has a body for all, which has yet to be. In Hebrews 10:5, as God prepared a body for Jesus Christ He has such a design for you.

The body which is not will be the body for the future. There will be a metamorphosis; the grub will be transformed into the beautiful. You have seen the worm crawl into the earth but wait until you see what appears! There is a miner at work in that earth and what goes in shrivelled and ugly will come out golden. From the old leather the golden slipper will appear, the grave will not decide the design, God will. From that same earth came the first Adam, beautifully, manfully, perfectly arranged.

We can arrange the funeral, the shape of the coffin, the headstone with the words written on it, and the flowers, but God arranges the new anatomy! Each one will be a Mr. Universe! The body is weak and, after Adam, is sown in dishonour. Sin has marred and corrupted us. Through the Body of Jesus, God has constructed something far better. All the words of better and best from the Book of Hebrews will be in this new form[3]. It is the difference between Jesus and Adam, the Heavenly and the earthly.

The builder of the new body

The botanical scientist produces new bodies constantly through the womb of mother nature, from old bulbs, seeds and, sometimes, apple cores or plum stones. There is an artistry at work in that which is left for dead.

The architect of the Heavenlies and of the ages has been at work. Jesus is described as the steward of the ages in Ephesians[4]. If God has done it for Isaac who was offered as a sacrifice and died in type, but was raised from the dead, He can do it again and again. Resurrections can be repeated forever. Hebrews 11:35 tells us that they received their loved ones back from the dead. They were looking for a more enduring substance. If God can and will raise one from the dead, He can raise everyone from the dead. Jesus is the firstfruits of them that slept[5], the firstborn[6], the first begotten[7]. Note the words, 'He is not here; He is risen'[8]. What God did through Jesus He will do for you. The Lord who can grow the first rose, light the first star, can also provide another body. Even a tent is another body, after the hide has been removed from the animal. Leather shoes are another body.

This body we have now is but a tent, sinews, muscle, fat and flesh with blood. Jesus referred to His body as a temple.[9] We are in a shack in a wilderness with creaking parts and swinging gates. We are known as strangers, foreigners, pilgrims, but we belong to the household of faith. As the years go by we degenerate into the faded picture, the tattered sheet, arriving as dust. We are as the child sent to school so well dressed yet arriving home with trousers torn, one shoe missing, coat swinging over the shoulder! There is character within, just as the ark, the golden candlestick and the table of shewbread was within the Tabernacle.[10]

Leaving behind the old body of humiliation

To die is to leave the old tattered garment of a body behind in cemetery and grave. It is the undertaker's coinage. We await a resurrection and a body, and the shape of what 'is' does not determine the beauty of what shall 'be'. From the same clay a variety of vessels are wrought by the potter. From one length of steel come so many varied designs — pins, brooches, poles. Redemption in Jesus provides a new body. Romans 8:38, 39 says that not even death can separate you from the love of God, nor height, nor depth — the depth of the grave. The grave is lined with the love of God. The shroud may have no pockets, but God has many things reserved in His pockets, one of which is Eternity. His hands are still at work. Our hands may be tied in death, but His hands operate forever in life.

To be absent from the body is to be present with the Lord, to be in a place awaiting a new resurrection body which moth and rust cannot corrupt, reserved, undefiled and never fading away. The thief cannot break through and steal, the gravedigger's shovel can neither cover or dig into it.[11] The eyes grow not dim, the teeth and hair do not fall out, the hearing needs no aid, the eyes no specs. The sunshine cannot stroke away its colour or beauty.

Where are we before we enter a new body?[12]

We do not sleep in the body in the grave, we are in the presence of the Lord.[13] God is a God of the living, not the sleeping or the dead. He is full of life. This life on earth is a valley of shadows but the life to come is the sunshine after the shadow. The liveliest and the loveliest place to be in the universe is with God. This is universal rest, universal peace.

Paul sees this body as a tent, while Jesus, in John 14:1–3, speaks of many mansions. Two totally different Greek words are used to define body and mansion. One has many rooms, the other has room for you. The contrast Paul uses is that while we are in this body we are absent from home. We can never be at home until we go home to be with the Lord. You can say, I am going home, or you can say, I am coming home. Even better, after death, to say, I am home. I will arise and go to My Father.

The promise of a new body

The earnest, the proof, the evidence, and sometimes the word describes the engagement ring, the piece of land given, the siezen, in old English, the spade full of dirt or a tuft of grass which proves ownership, belongs to the believer in the gift of the Holy Spirit. 2 Corinthians 5:5 calls it a guarantee. The Holy Spirit is the guarantor and the guarantee. The guarantee is not the object but the pledge for safe keeping of the object, even as sacks of goods were sealed until they reached the required destination.

Our modern security transport vehicles are sealed with seals of lead. Abraham gave silver for the land in which he buried Sarah.[14] That silver, as Christ's redemption which was purchased with His blood, is your guarantee of life after death. It is God's down payment, engagement ring, promising future glory. We, like Israel seeking out the promised land, have but tasted of the grapes of Eschol. The best is yet to be. It is victory after venture.

It will be a body of glory

Redemption covers body, soul and spirit. The redemption of the body is part of the package of salvation. When the Roman child was adopted it was publicly dressed in the clothes and insignia of the new family. The old clothes were taken away, even as your old body will be removed. The new body, as new clothes, will be yours.[15]

When we die we pass from this body of bones and flesh into the presence of the Lord and the prayer of Jesus in John 17:24, is answered. We have glorious bodies which are to be like the resurrection body of Jesus Christ. We are where the glory of Jesus, His eternal glory, His pre-incarnation glory, and after-redemption glory is seen as it lights up all Eternity. We shall witness first hand all the workings of His glory as seen in the Church and revealed in Heaven. As we saw in factory visits from school when the raw materials were turned into rare and beautiful forms — old glass, broken, smashed or chipped — re-appeared in fine designs and the most ornate glass objects. If we see Eternity in the light of His glory then all will be seen, heard, known and enjoyed.

The new body will be a permanent body

2 Corinthians 5:1 says we have a building, not simply a body. The difference is, the writer wants to add strength and actuality to what you will have. It could be called a body building. A different Greek word is used for this new state. It is strongly constructed. The foundation is deep for it was laid before the foundation of the world and it is built to last for ever. That new body is God's final abiding place for you, a forever body, eternal in the heavens, formed and illuminated as any star set in the sky.

2 Corinthians 5:2, a house; verse 8, present with the Lord. It means to be in one's own country as if after some journey abroad where customs are different to those at home. It suggests to be among one's own people. Heaven will be populated in God's presence. Never again will it be recorded, 'He went out from the presence of the Lord.' That presence and promise provide everything. While you are in your earthly house you are absent from your body, just as the grub is absent from the body of the majestic butterfly. That which crawled along on legs, will fly. An egg laid in slime becomes an exquisite dragonfly with many colours glistening in the light of the sun.

This 'present with the Lord' places the believer among those who share the same thoughts, deeds and language. It is a word which is related to a king and is to belong to your own tongue, tribe and nation. I will dwell in the house of the Lord forever. Your summer residence awaits you. The architect is still planning, still working on it and there we become part of one great family. While here on earth there is a part missing, the complete will only be when each person takes up residence. That better half, that sunny side, the real you will be revealed in God's presence. Home is where you are really yourself, where you feel at home, where the real values are.

2 Corinthians 5:1 says this new body is for a new abode, one not made with hands. When astronauts go into another sphere they have the necessary equipment for the purpose. A fish needs such a body for water, as a whale does. Corn seed needs that type of body for the soil and for germination. The chief characteristic of this new formation is that of eternal life. The very wholeness of God will be exhibited through these bodies. God in His wisdom, not in evolution, has provided this body, the body of glory. The body is provided for an atmosphere and for the environment of perfection.

That body is God's masterpiece

When traders want to show their wares they book hotel rooms and call in friends to show them what they have. The market is for the purpose of displaying the wares. God will use the whole of eternity. You are His treasured possession. He has no other plans but those found in your new body.

The Sunday School teacher was telling the class all about Heaven. Sarah's dad had gone to Devon to play golf, and when asked if they wanted to say anything, little Sarah's hand shot up, 'My daddy has gone to Heaven', she said, and, to the wonderment of the class, added, 'but he's coming back on Monday!'

Heaven will be such a display of God's presence and power, the power and the glory in the plan forever and ever. Here and now you are living to die. In Eternity you will be living, not as a continuation of what you have now. It is not this life added to or lengthened, it will be a quality of life uniquely different, diffused to every part where thought and wish immediately become deed, where desire becomes destiny.

This body of flesh must be dissolved, the pins and the cords removed and it must return to the dust. That is expressed in the word dissolved. Each constituent part returning to its own. From dust you are and to dust you will return. We believe in a redemption body of glory. There is an earthly body and there is an Heavenly body. There is that terrestial and there is that celestial. We all wear different outfits to suit different occasions. This new body, the resurrection body, will be the latest design in living! The greatest clothes show you have ever seen will take place, with you as a model, displaying all the handiwork of God. Jesus is going to be admired and praised in us.[16]

It will be a fashionable body

What is groan and moan, mud and mire, must be turned into glory. The shattered and tattered made up into something permanent, woven from top to bottom without any adjoining seam. Rags of mortality will be replaced with the beauties of glory. The wool taken from the back of the sheep and, by a process of cleaning, spinning, combing and dyeing, is transformed into another body. From the nakedness of the shower to the clothing of the wardrobe. God knows that which will suit the occasion. He is the tailor and has cut the pattern according to the cloth. It is more than clothing with cloth, it is the clothing with a body, and not only clothing but wrought gold. You will be raised as a Phoenix out of the ashes, as a silver-winged dove flying high. The same words will be used as when they saw Jesus perform miracles: 'We have never seen it on this fashion. He does all things well.'[17]

The new body has been typified

A lovely picture of the resurrection as we receive a new body is the picture of Eve being taken from the side of Adam as he slept. A new body from an old body. A future body arose from the sleeping form. Where was Eve before God gave her a body?

During His earthly ministry Jesus was constantly creating resurrection faculties. To the blind man he gave new eyes; a new hand in place of a stunted hand; the dead were certainly raised; new ears, new speech, to those deaf and mute. He found Legion among the tombs and put a right mind within him. The prodigal son in Luke 15 returned and a new coat was placed upon him, shoes on his feet. During the earthly ministry of Jesus every faculty, every part of the body was restored, in different places and at different times. He will do the same in the resurrection but on a grand scale. Those things Ezekiel witnessed in the valley of dry bones when a great army stood on its feet, Jesus will do for all believers.[18]

As Jonathan gave his garments to David, the future King, so Jesus will do for you, dear reader, but then it will be a body.

God can create any number of bodies and all types

Think of all the human bodies which have come after the body of Adam. Balance that by considering all the new bodies provided for in Jesus Christ. In the Book of Revelation John sees them as ten thousand times ten thousand and thousands of thousands, and as if that is not enough he adds a number which no man could number.[19] The creative ability of God is endless and still there is more.

A gentleman gave a suit to Billy Bray, the Cornish evangelist and told him, 'The Lord told me to give this to you. Does it fit?' Billy replied, 'If the Lord told you to give it to me, it will fit!' Every body will fit.

Believing will lead to receiving a new body

We walk by faith not by sight but then sight will give us what faith believed for. As the Holy Spirit formed the body of Jesus in the womb of a virgin, so shall that same Holy Spirit do with believers, not with hands but by God, the One who created the first body. It will be a repeated success, the Rolls Royce of the skies! The voice which uttered the words 'Let there be light' will say, Let there be a body!

Nature calls forth new bodies for different reasons and seasons

Every springtime there is another clothing. Spring calls, new bodies appear as if from nowhere, created by nature. God will be the One at work for us. Not a change of clothing from summer to winter but a change of bodily construction. This body of death and weakness, this frailty that is ready to fragment will become a new body of life, eternal in the heavens. One word in the Russian language means both 'stay' and 'live'.

This body is a continuing construction

There is a contrast between the Tabernacle, tent and the Temple building. Such a contrast is between the body which is a tent now, and the more secure and forever building to be housed in the presence of the Lord. There was a certain glory in the Old Testament ritual. John says, 'We beheld His glory'[20]. That is a living body. The whole of creation declares His handiwork, and becomes the pulpit of His glory. Your new body will be His shop window.

The business of earth will find true rest in Heaven. The pilgrim's staff will be replaced by the golden rod of the King. Heaven is happiness. Heaven is home, a haven. The saviour is to be replaced by the Lord, the Lamb by the Lion. There is a presence to enter into. Even the souls under the altar in the Book of Revelation have voices to call out.[21] All the features of your physical frame are intrinsically linked with the future.

You will not be without a body

The very term 'naked' as found in 2 Corinthians 5:3 was used by the Greeks of naked spirits without a body. Paul's words, his challenge is that we shall not be found unclothed. There will be such a completeness. There will be no floating spirits in Heaven.

You will be at home, to be among one's own people, not to travel abroad, to have enough in that which surrounds to make you want to stay and stare.

John 14:3 says, 'I will receive you unto myself.' Literally, it is 'I shall take you along to My own home.' You will have a house as a body but I too will have a place for that body to find fullness of expression. Absent from the body and present with the Lord. Absent — out from one's people; present — to be back among those people, not spirits or shadowy forms. Dr. Strong comments[22] that the word absent means to emigrate. It is present with the Lord. It is one who is in his own place or land.

Where do you belong? To whom do you belong? The ship has come to port; the star has appeared in the sky; the utensil placed back in the rack where it was always meant to be. The silver piece has been found and restored, even as the sheep in the parables (Luke 15). We have been abroad, on safari, but now the Master has returned to take up residence in His rightful mansion.

The new body is to be at home

The Greek word for home is 'endemeo'. To be at home and to stay at home. Home Sweet Home. Where I live, think, speak and have my being, where I am known, where space is made for me.

We must not judge health by a sick body, nor must we judge what shall be by what is present at this moment. There may be a struggling saint who is having a grim time of living, but do not judge the life that shall be by the life that is known now. There is to be another quality and form of life. The quintessence of the quiet life will be quite a life. The last time I saw that lovely red apple it was but a flower head, with a bee entering into it, letting the blossom be both workshop and factory. What a change as it developed! Such a change will be ours! For some it will happen in a moment, in the twinkling of an eye; for others it will be a resting in the presence of the Lord.

There came a day when I travelled from London to Doncaster, returning home from Theological College. The old steam engine was worn out and seemed to take light years to complete the journey. Later, when I took the same journey back after the holiday, the engine had been replaced with a bright gleaming object that could pull anything, and go on and on forever! The electric train had arrived! Travelling through life, do not mistake station for destination!

There is a preparation for receiving the new body

During the course of this life you have been at school. I don't know what grade has been achieved, but I do know that you are going on to higher education, when you will know all things. The very quality of future life is perfection, that which has been broken and is incomplete will be completed. The scribbling of the child will become the masterpiece of the artist. When you returned from school everything was prepared by those who cared for you. When we leave this classroom, this life of training, there will be that which is already prepared for them that love Him.

Let love for Him bring you to Him so that one day you might go to be with Him forever. Believe on the Lord Jesus Christ. Live in Jesus. Be reminded that every trial, every dark cloud, every mishap, has a heart of gold in that there is teaching before reaching. God is making you as big as you can be in love, faith, trust, kindness, and wholeness to ensure that you will feel at home in this new engineering of Eternity, the body of Resurrection and glory. 'We want our transitory life to be absorbed in the life that is Eternal' (Phillips translation of 2 Corinthians 5:4).

NOTES

1. 1 Corinthians 15:29.
2. 1 Corinthians 13:12.
3. Hebrews 1:4; 7:7,19,22; 8:6; 9:23.
4. Ephesians 1:10; 3:2.
5. 1 Corinthians 15:20.
6. Colossians 1:18.
7. Romans 8:29.
8. Luke 24:6.
9. John 2:19.
10. Hebrews 9:2–21.
11. 1 Peter 1:4.
12. 2 Corinthians 5:8.
13. See previous chapter on this topic.
14. Genesis 23:15,16.
15. Romans 8:23.
16. Ephesians 1:12.
17. Mark 2:12.
18. Ezekiel 37:1–7.
19. Revelation 5:11.
20. John 1:14.
21. Revelation 6:9,10.
22. See Dr. James Strong, *Concordance of the Bible*.

Will Future Life Be Better Than This Life?

In Philippians 1:21–30, the writer, Paul the Apostle, sets out his convictions about life after death. In verse 23, he states 'It will be far better.' Whatever has been the best in this life, there is a superlative awaiting you. The expectation will not be cut off, it will be totally fulfilled.

If Paul had written to the Philippians that the future life, the departure of the soul into the presence of God, was better, that would have been as a shaft of light or ray of sunshine passing through a dark, dreary Roman cell. Joy would have been complete. We could have rejoiced in that which was better, yet what is coming from the pen of the Apostle is not that it is good or a little better, but it is the best of all. We know which suit, which dress, is the best one. The best days of life are marked out as 'red letter' days. This phrase was taken from religious calendars which had feast days and holidays marked out in red. Take the best of everything — and it can still be bettered! The best is by comparison. A person can play the flute well, until they hear James Last play! You might have poetic inspiration not yet discovered, until you read Alfred Lord Tennyson, Rudyard Kipling or William Shakespeare!

The best is yet to be

In Luke 15:22, when the prodigal returned, he was given a coat, the best robe, the robe reserved for special occasions. Compared with his tattered garments and his mean existence the best was yet to be. The comparison here is not that which is better but that which is far better. How long is the stretch of your mind? How far will it curve? Can it stretch beyond the elastic or the circle stage? There is such a stretch that cannot be measured when we compare life as we have known it with life that shall be in the future. It is the expanse, the difference between Heaven and earth, earth and hell. It is the paper boat in comparison to the Ark Royal, the work of origami with that of the master architect.

That future is the country you will love the best

Oswald J. Smith, Pastor of The People's Church in Canada, wrote a book entitled *The Country I Love Best*. In it he compared countries, nations, places and people, but the best place is to be with the Lord. The best life of all is the life of God, after death. Who wants a garden in a box when they can have a forest or parkland?

To be with Christ is far better. It is further than the furthest, better than the best. It is described in the wine of John 2:10, where the best wine was set before them at the end rather than at the beginning. This superlative language is used to describe a superlative place. We are familiar with the phrase, 'You've tried the rest, now try the best.' The best is yet to be! Your best years are the eternal years. Maturity in this life will find its completion in the majesty of future life. Your future days are never final days, they are your finest days, filled with golden hours, majestic moments, silver seconds, where all yearnings will be fulfilled. The future is something to look forward to.

When Greek writers or orators were attempting to interest readers or listeners, they used a great word as a foundational word and turned it into a functional word. If a great word was used at the beginning then what followed wasn't too important. Then, when they had adopted a word which contained a whole world of thinking, as if taking a thread of silk or cotton, they would weave a whole statement, or write a letter around that one word. This lonely one word was married to other lesser words and would thus attract attention and keep that attention until they had received the whole of the matter. Their congregations behaved as troops facing a commander, as if on parade, as actions followed the word of command.

The writer to the Hebrews does this in the opening verses, Hebrews 1:1–3: 'God who at "sundry times" and in "diverse manners",' in many parts and in many ways. He uses a great word to introduce a sublime idea.

The writer to the Philippians presents the simple word as a sample word, the word 'better'. It is not a word which can be measured because the word 'far' is added to the word 'better'. This word 'better' becomes succinct, that which underpins and undergirds everything else he has to say about life after death. As the tent maker with a stitch, so he pulls it all together in one word. It is as if one was tasting dishes, comparing them to the experiences of life and marking out the one which has to be tasted in the future with the words 'far better'. In any horticultural show there are many flowers, vegetables and preserves that are marked with the word 'reserved'. Only one wins the show. There may be one which wins in every class.

Ephesians 3:20 says 'He is able to do exceeding abundantly above all' — that which passes knowledge. When we consider what God has prepared it can be the comparison between the straw on the floor and the block of gold, the broken-down shack or the palace, old fashioned ideas and modern inventions. From the Gospel of better things comes that which is far better. When the works and miracles of Jesus were compared with the religion of the Pharisees the people said, 'We never saw it on this fashion.'[1]

The promise of a better future came from a dismal background

From where did we receive the Philippian Epistle of joy, or Ephesians and Colossians, which contain the greatest revelations of the New Testament? They came from a prison cell in Rome! Those Epistles are considered far better than the rest, and future life is far better than this life. As different as the life the prodigal son experienced in Luke 15, whilst in the pigsty and the far country, compared with what he received in Father's house; the difference in the life of the wandering sheep on the hillside among wolves and the life it had when it was placed on the shoulders of the shepherd and brought home rejoicing. It is the difference between having a little oil and being an oil magnate! Whatever you are or have in this life, the Gospel of Jesus Christ offers something more that can be measured in two small words, 'far better'.

As a child when in my childhood mind I could not measure distance or time, I was simply told that it was 'far' and would take a long time to arrive.

To all who are Christ's, it is far better. It has not yet entered into the heart of man what God has prepared for them that love Him. Part of it has been revealed and received by the Spirit of God.[2] Your wildest dreams, your deepest thoughts, your greatest visions and strongest desires will be bettered. We need hope to bring us through. Jesus had a crown of thorns before He had a crown of gold. Gold prospectors must dig before they find the gold. There may be a period of suffering through which you must pass before you enter into that which is far better.

Some things are better in quality, rather than quantity

Some things are better because of choice. The value placed on them makes them better, better made, better crafted, better painted, better adorned and arranged. This better future life is not a matter of choice, it stands as the better life awaiting you as fact. It will be far better when compared with the views of earth's strata. The scenery will be better. Some things are better because of the process through which they have passed, the years of waiting, waiting that provides maturing and heightens the appreciation.

The man who wrote the words, 'It is far better,' knew of comparisons. He had travelled, he was an educated man, recognised as having sat at the feet of Gamaliel. Missionary journeys were part of his routine.

For Roman cobbled roads there will be streets of gold. No broken stump of the tree but palm trees and the Tree of Life. Instead of the broken down cottages, the rows of tents brought to Paul the tent maker for repair, there will be mansions above. Elijah's chariot was better than travelling on foot. The Roman Triumphs were nothing compared to this life over the edge, death's dividing line. This is not Paul's appeal to Caesar but to God.

It will be like the man who said to visitors, 'Come into my garden, and I will show you my roses.' One day he fell in love and he so admired the beauty of his lady that he said to her, 'Come into my garden and let my roses see you!'

The writer listened, learned, watched. He experienced and experimented and then he wrote these words. In Ephesians 6, he took the Roman soldier and his armour, likening it to Christian armour. That is why he stamped every word and scene with the word 'better'. He heard of famous battles, wars, conquests of new countries and the numbers of those subjugated by the Roman Empire. They spoke of gladiators and famous victories. Heaven will be as the story of the natives who, when converted, compared witnessing and winning souls to the taking of scalps! Heaven will be a place of famous stories, great deeds and final conquests. Much of what will be discussed has yet to be written. Your heart is the notepad!

Every blast on the Roman trumpet might herald Paul's departure. He is keenly listening for another trumpet sound, found in 1 Thessalonians 4:17. When he was taken to the cells he did not know what awaited him on earth, but he had assurance of that which awaited him in Heaven. They could never destroy his hope, nor could they extinguish his desire for God. Every time the door was unlocked it could mean the releasing of his soul to something better than chains, more than bright shining armour, to the circle of angels clothed in white.

Paul could make many comparisons before he reached the best

Many times he was disturbed from his sleep by the sound of the trumpet, the marching of feet, the shouts of war and the changing of the guard, but there will be harmonious sounds of deep, prolonged worship where one voice blends with another until the whole is in harmony, the harmony of many waters, of many becoming one. No more bruising by the Roman guards, no more harsh language, no more cries of pain. Every discordant sound will be turned into a note of pure music. Old tapes and records used on modern machines remove all the blips and scratches. One voice, the voice of the Archangel, 1 Thessalonians 4:17, will sound out the Resurrection from the dead.[3]

Whatever happens it will be far better than the dark grave. To hear the voice of Elijah as he calls the fire down! To hear the shout of Joshua as he goes towards the doomed city! All will be seen. The rabble will be turned into a choir. The food will be part of all manner of fruit yielded each month for the hungry mouth.[4] He will have some of the hidden manna[5]. No more stale bread or stagnant water, never to be wrapped in old sheepskin again. He need make no request for books, parchment or coat.[6]

All will be fully taken care of. The naked and the destitute, the insane and the sick will be visited, clothed and found in their right mind. Deep longings and desires will be adequately fulfilled. Every hungry mouth filled with fulness. Heaven's crumbs are better than the loaves of earth! The wedding feast comes into its true festive spirit. Think of it, name it, then add to it the words 'far better'.

When the world boasts of gilded toys, when the pride of life seems to be the only thing that is really worshipped, think on these things. Modern technology will be outdated by a million millennia!

The future contains all that is best

The body which Paul possessed, his wracked, painful, weak eyes and twisted nose, will be changed into a body like unto His glorious body.[7] This body of humiliation, he writes from his prison cell, will be from prison to praise, and from prison to palace in the words 'far better'. This body of humiliation will become a glorious body. For pain, pearl; for stiffness and deadness, the freedom of Eternity. Heaven is the Best. The saying 'they have gone to a better place', will be completed. There is more height, depth, breadth and length in that which has been prepared as Love's Feast.

Even that which is revealed in Scripture is but a dark glass with a certain fogginess about it. My mind is as the eye with a patch over it when I consider the future without the words 'far better'. I am as one trying to see beyond what cannot be seen until arrival. We have come many times to the Scriptures, arriving as blind Bartimaeus to receive sight and light about the future, expecting honey, only to find solid rock, until the words 'far better' have rolled away the stone. Better than a bed of sickness, better than a blind eye, better than being so cold that Carpus is requested to bring the cloak with him.[8] Better than Churches, better than stained glass windows, better than any Church or believer scattered throughout Asia Minor.

In the future they and us will be altogether with the Altogether Lovely. There will be no loneliness in Heaven. The island will be part of the whole man. No man will be an island unto himself. You will have so much to offer, so much to give, and so much will be received. Loneliness and isolation will be like a foreign tongue, for all will speak the same language. The 'far better' will be far better than any of the most glorious Empires. Nobody did it quite like Rome. The best robe from the prodigal son, the best wine from the wedding at Cana in Galilee, will be added. As in 2

Kings 10:3, the best and the meekest of your master's sons will be there. Esther will be there, she who was preferred above the best.[9] Every person will be part of the innumerable company.[10]

The rest will be replaced by the best

The Roman prison doors will be replaced by pearly gates and Paul would be surrounded by angels. Instead of Caesar's edicts, there will be the throne of God. He will be a citizen of Heaven, a denizen of grace. The coarse language is changed into the silver oratory of angels. Bring in the massed choir, let them sing unto and into all Eternity! The warmth of this promise and the presence of Christ will light a fire that will burn day and night within Paul's heart, maintaining the spiritual glow.[11] These chains, 'I would that every man was as I am except for these chains!' Yet they will be turned into medals received and become the embrace of the jewellery of Heaven.

Samuel Rutherford, one of the godly men of Scotland referred to his chains, when he was imprisoned for wanting to preach the true Gospel, as Christ's jewels.

From the cursing of the soldier to the blessing of God! Whatever you have now, the future will be a step up, a step in and a step forward into something greater, more glorious than any of the lights of earth.[12]

The exact Greek translation of 'far better' is 'far more, better'. Dying is a healing, a getting better from the worst curse that this world has ever known. Do not say, 'I am dying,' but 'I am getting better.' Palm trees and flowing rivers make better resting places than cold prison cells. It is much better than tongue can tell, brain can think, or eye can see. The mind becomes heavy and dull, it needs sparkle, a new thought, another idea.

You may think now that Paul wrote great letters and epistles, but wait until you hear him speak in Heaven! Wait until you see what he can write with a new mind that will be part of his new body! Whilst in a Philippian jail he sang, and that produced something of an earthquake, but wait until you hear the notes he can reach in the glory!

Artists and early writers describe Paul as being short, of short legs and with a large nose, weatherbeaten and not a pleasant face.[13] He is described by the Corinthian believers as not having a strong bodily presence. That will be changed! He will have something far better.

There is the superlative found in that which is far better

The theme of the New Jerusalem will continue as long as God shall endure. The best is to be bettered, to have something more added. Shaken together, running over, after being pressed down!

A dying man said, 'I am sinking. No; I am dying. No, I am living!' Here is healing. When I have gone, tell them I am altogether better!

The dreams of every Joseph will come true. The vision will become a reality. There is to be the betterment of a man changing one set of circumstances for another, but more than that, the man himself is changed. The dull seed becomes the flower, the coal the diamond. You will be different. The great change will come. It is not just a continuation of a trouble free life but life on another scale with new dimensions.

The word 'better' is only a small word, a comparative word, yet in it we find all the areas of choice and joy, reminding us of a parable of Jesus in which He said, 'and last of all he sent His Son unto them'.[14] There is nothing final about this. There is a future which is better and that betterment commences as we allow Jesus to make us into better people of God. Better, because Jesus is there and He is the best. Better, because you will know as you are known. Better, as you will find the word 'better' in the Book of Hebrews some seven times. It will be more than seven times better than the Old Covenant. The New Covenant is just that! Better, because you will inherit all things, prepared by your Father from the beginning of creation.[15] What a good work He made of His creation but how much more delightful will be His new arrangements. Wedding arrangements are always better than funeral arrangements on earth, but here the order will be reversed!

The vision of a better future

Who is the Beloved? Is He your Beloved? He is the Altogether Lovely.[16] That says it all. Out of the loveliness of Jesus Christ, this loveliness appears. It is darling to all those who are in love with Love. One major world language has some eighty words which express the word 'darling'. In surrendering to Him I surrender to everything He is and has to offer me, in time and Eternity. As far above and beyond other men as Jesus Christ was and is, so the future will be that which is rarer and more pure than anything ever known.

Paul has gazed on the Roman Generals. He has looked on all around him, sometimes with a microscopic eye, but now he gazes with telescopic eye. There the guards stand back, the wall opens before him and he sees beyond the immediate. The barrier is removed. Like John on Patmos, the door is opened. At one time he was caught up into the Third Heaven, Paradise.[17] He cannot utter what he heard, but he can tell what he saw and it was far better. As the spies going into the land of Canaan, Paul says, we are well able to possess it, for it is a better land. Everything is bigger, better. In that land are great grapes, and giants.

Many stories are being told in the prison. They speak of the glories of war and the magnificence of Rome, but it all dims when this prisoner begins to tell of the triumphs of Christianity. That is not all, he says, wait until you get into the life beyond and hear all the wondrous stories of grace. It will be better than anything you have ever heard!

The gnostics and philosophers all said there was something better — but Paul it was who said, 'far better'. The dream must become a reality. The far off land must be walked upon. The world wants Heaven, but it is the Heaven of their own making and choosing. They want the best without salvation and the Gospel, choosing to go their own way to Heaven. There will always be a need for that which is far better.

That which is far better awaits you as you join the journey to the skies, through the Milky Way, by the Great Bear, through the Southern Cross and all the other constellations, into the presence of God.

Dying is living.

NOTES

1. Mark 2:12.
2. 1 Corinthians 2:9,10.
3. This will take place when Jesus comes again.
4. Revelation 2:7; 22:2.
5. Revelation 2:17.
6. 2 Timothy 4:13.
7. Philippians 3:21.
8. 2 Timothy 4:13.
9. Esther 2:9.

10. Revelation 20:8.
11. Romans 12:11, fervent in spirit.
12. Acts 16:29.
13. Josephus, the Roman historian.
14. Mark 12:5–8.
15. Matthew 25:34.
16. Song of Solomon 5:9.
17. 2 Corinthians 12:4.

Other books by the same author:

Paths of Righteousness in Psalm 23
The Growing Pains of Peter
In Sickness and in Health

All obtainable from New Living Publishers.